White Light, Yellow Light, Districts, Dynamics:

The Socioeconomic Divide

by L. Tommy Long

DORRANCE
PUBLISHING CO
EST. 1920
PITTSBURGH, PENNSYLVANIA 15238

Dorrance Publishing Co
585 Alpha Drive
Pittsburgh, PA 15238
Visit our website at *www.dorrancebookstore.com*

ISBN: 978-1-6491-3504-9
eISBN: 978-1-6491-3921-4

This book is dedicated to Joe Scarborough and the entire *Morning Joe* broadcast for their advocacy of "Speaking Truth to Power." Although speaking truth to power is not a recent edict, my inspiration for its usage is a direct response to its advocacy by *Morning Joe* on MSNBC.

I have long been frustrated with the apathy of the working class for the political process, and I have pondered ways to reach as many as possible to offer encouragement and provide a vehicle to help people take control of their own eventuality. Through this book, my hope is to "speak truth to power" by exposing the false narratives and dishonest and insulting discourse of those in power and by offering solutions that will enable the working class to understand and harness its power. Decidedly, those in power (those with financial prowess) control the narrative. Throughout history, those who control the financial institutions, in every epoch, control all other institutions. Derivatively, they control what we are taught in schools, what we believe constitutes a balanced diet, what we believe to be acceptable religious groups, what we think of as good medicine, what is right for the family unit, what is legal or illegal, etc.

The number one thing that they control that helps to control us is the narrative. Those in power always seek to control the narrative or retelling of something that happened. Hence, the narrative is not the story itself, but rather the retelling of the story. A retelling of a story in a manner in which they want you to see it is not the real or complete story. This is referred to as a false narrative, and it misrepresents the truth, the whole truth, and nothing but the truth.

Hence, a narrative and the truth are sharply distinguished. By derivation, just because someone has the ability to control the narrative does not mean that they are telling the truth necessarily. For example, there is dispositive evidence that President Trump encouraged foreign governments to interfere in our elections, but President Trump has convinced many that he did nothing by repeatedly tweeting and saying to every audience "no collusion." Although he is an avatar of disgust, his lack of integrity and his penchant for lying make him masterful at controlling the narrative. He lies uncontrollably and projects his shortcomings onto others. If we are indeed "what we repeatedly do," as Aristotle said, then President Trump is a liar, full stop! Admittedly, some think it is too harsh to label the President a liar, but this President routinely engages in name-calling and labeling of his political opponents and anyone else who disagrees with him about anything. Besides, if we allow the most powerful voice in the world to get away with repeatedly saying things that are not true, we will materially diminish our ability to "speak truth to power."

Contents

Introduction
A Call for the Exercising of Critical Thought

When thinking about any matter so as to reach a sound decision, an objective analysis of the facts is critical before formulating a position of judgment. When we totally rely upon information presented to us, which is generally lacking the rational, skeptical, unbiased analysis, or evaluation of factual evidence, we are easily bamboozled. If you're like most everyone else, generally you look for easy answers that don't require critical thought. Much of our reliance on easy answers is the result of time constraints, but not entirely. Unfortunately, much of it is due to our own laziness or apathy. Since the incipiency of this democratic republic, most of us have not participated in the democratic process that determines how our lives are governed. For many years, a large majority (blacks and women) were prohibited from participating in any political process. There has been substantial sacrifice and blood shed on behalf of the disenfranchised so that all American citizens can participate. Our demonstrated lack of appreciation raised questions about the efficacy of such sacrifice. It is therefore shameful that many of us are too lazy or apathetic to spend the necessary time to stay informed and use our own critical thought as the impetus for our political decisions.

There are many benefits from developing critical thinking skills, e.g., better control of what you learn and increased tolerance for the views of others.

All working-class people, liberal or conservative, want the opportunity for upward mobility in the society in which they live, but we are not always willing to put forth the effort to critically think about what is necessary to make that opportunity an eventuality.

According to the 2010 Census, the number of Americans who were of voting age comprised 194.3 million: 62.9 percent of the total population. Despite an increase of over eight million citizens in the eligible population, turnout declined from 131 million voters in 2008 to an estimated 126 million voters in 2012. More than 68 million Americans did not even participate in the process, and many of those who did voted against their own best interests as a result of the failure to think critically about which candidates most align with the issues that are important to them. The voter turnouts for the mid-term elections are even more egregious because most of us don't even know who our local candidates are or where they stand on any particular issue. By derivation, we help in electing diabolical self-servants rather than public servants.

~~~

PICTURE YOURSELF IN ANY OF THESE DREADFUL CATEGORIES:

We all fall short; some to a greater or lesser extent than others, but we can all do much more than we are currently doing to effectuate change. Apathy is one of the maladies of modern society, but now it is essential that we all show concern. When we fail to fully participate, we are failing ourselves, our families, and our communities.

How many among you have been in court for a simple traffic violation or some other minor offense where the judge disrespected you as a human being? Did you leave calling him/her names and thinking he/she should not be in that position because they exuded an abuse of power; or did you complain in some other way? President Obama famously and frequently said "don't complain; VOTE," and I agree with that sentiment. Municipal judges are elected officials charged with the responsibility for meting out justice according to statutes. Yet, many of their judgements are without the benefit of whether it's a construence in consideration of "statutory construction?" Any question of statutory construence or interpretation begins with looking at the plain language of the statute to discover its original intent. To discover a statute's original intent, courts are supposed to first look to the words of the statute and apply their usual and ordinary meanings. Rather, judges tend to allow their own personal beliefs to enter into their decision making. Therefore, their implicit biases become part of their judgement. We must start voting them out when they are unfit or fail in their responsibilities in such a common sense manner. By so doing, we will be less solicitous of electing such judges, and we will eventually elect public servants that actually serve us and not look at us condescendingly. Respect and common courtesy are essential qualities for people in elected offices. We must treat them with respect, and they must give nothing less in return.

The real problem is that our lack of critical thought paralyzes our every action to participate in a meaningful way that will truly benefit us. Derivatively, we accept the egregious lies told to us by those running for office, but more especially those who have been elected to office. With even a small amount of research, we would see the disparities in what they say and what they do. If we cannot trust what they say, they don't deserve our votes. We don't need politicians to pass legislation for term limits because we have that within our control. If we elect someone to office and they don't do what we elected them to do, then it is incumbent upon us to not send them there for another term. The answer, then, is to stop caterwauling or crying and just give critical thought to the voting process on every level. Stop electing and re-electing the same oleaginous characters time and time again. It might take several permutations to rid ourselves of the self-serving "public servants," but it will be time well spent. Personally, I was apathetic about fully participating in the process, but I can now say, without equivocation, that my life has been appreciably more fulfilling since I began full engagement. I posit that you will experience a similar sense of accomplishment if you indulge yourself in this new way of thinking. Yet change is not without cost.

It is misguided and bad felicific calculus to suggest that any of this is easy, but if we are willing to pay the price, then we can change the entire political landscape in a way that will be beneficial to the entire population. However, if we continue to omit critical thought from the process, we will continue to make only incremental gains, and in many instances experience socioeconomic regression. Furthermore, the old idiom "a wink is as good as a nod to a blind mule" applies to all who are not willing to think critically about whom and what we are voting for. In colloquial terms, without critical thought we are at the mercy of whatever someone wants to tell us.

Education is the most powerful weapon that you can use to make change, but education takes time and effort. Is that cost too high of a price for us to pay for a more suitable place in the socioeconomic fight in which we are immersed? One example is to educate yourself on the difference between a wage and a living wage: In 2018 the Department of Health and Human Services set the federal poverty level at $24,600 for a family of four. That's equivalent to $11.83 per hour for a full-time worker. A worker making the minimum wage of $7.35 per hour would be well below the poverty level. Many people have to work multiple jobs to earn a living wage. By derivation, the unemployment numbers do not tell the whole story, and people who live in that realm know that all too well. For example, the variables used by our government as indicators of a good economy—gross domestic product (GDP)—stock market rate—unemployment rate—are not at all indicative of a good economy for most Americans. Most Americans do not own stocks, and the unemployment rate is misleading for a number of reasons; one of which is that people who work for a wage less than $15 per hour are required to work another job to create a living wage. Therefore, by any serious analysis, the underemployment rate and the number of jobs held by each person must be included as two of the economic indicators. Clearly there are many more indicators we need to consider. For example, consumer spending is largely an indication of how much money poor people are spending; yet poor people, while earning less, have to spend all of what they earn due to the economic determinants designed into the economic system to create inequities for the poor.

Critically thinking about such matters as these is therefore essential, but there is a gap in education today whereby grades are valued more than learning. Model answers will get you the highest marks and critical and creative thinking get pushed aside. Be mindful not to get caught in the grade trap, but rather understand that the more you think critically about problems, the more likely it is that you can come up with new and more effective and efficient ways to solve said problems. Our focus in this book is to get you to think critically about political matters of the socioeconomic divide. So, let's turn up the lights (pun intended) on the white light, yellow light districts of the socioeconomic divide.

Chapter One
Disparate Districts

Let's start with the elephant in the room. The white light and yellow light districts are a real, physical thing that exist in every major city in America. Rural America, where there is no lighting to speak of, is largely associated with the yellow light districts. There are several reasons why this dynamic exists, but the two most notable are the difference in operational cost and the more obvious difference in illumination levels. I would posit that most people in the yellow light districts (low income communities) have never even given much thought to why their neighborhoods look different at night than the neighborhoods of the more affluent. Worse yet, many in the yellow light districts haven't even noticed this distinct lighting difference. Juxtaposed, those in the white light districts would, even if they did not know why, question the inferior quality of lighting in their neighborhoods. To whom should we direct our questioning? That is key in this scenario. The answer of course is the elected city officials in our municipality. Do you know who your city council members are? Have you ever attended a city council meeting? If we showed up in mass at every meeting, we could enact change that would make a difference in our neighborhoods.

In the yellow light districts, there are streets in the neighborhoods where it might take you ten minutes to enter onto a main thoroughfare at certain hours of the day. In the white light districts, there are traffic lights at similar thoroughfare entrances. The inhabitants of those districts attend city council meetings and lobby for traffic lights and anything else that they think will make life easier and safer in their neighborhoods. We must do the exact same thing, or we have little cause for complaining among ourselves. Moreover, it's of no benefit to us to complain among ourselves. Our assiduities and devoted or solicitous attention are essential to our progress.

If we attend city council meetings and make requests, but nothing ever changes, then we exercise our power to voting in every local election. Stop electing the same people to represent us if they fail to serve us in the same way they serve those in the white light districts. President Obama said during his presidential campaign, "Don't boo…VOTE!" Understand the power you possess by voting in every election and by attending every city council meeting that you can so that you are aware of the issues and can make informed decisions about whom and what you are voting for. This is my personal political approach that strives to appeal to ordinary people who feel that their concerns are disregarded by public officials established and funded by elite groups. The eventuality is that we must become informed voters who are full-time participants in the process and who make decisions based on common sense—reasonable grounds for doing, thinking, or feeling something. Political dissonance, the dissonance between what we are told and what we see with our own eyes, defies common sense or good judgement. There is no more of a glaring example of that than the electing of Donald J. Trump, an obvious demagogue, as President. According to the *Oxford English Dictionary*, a demagogue is a leader who gains popularity by exploiting prejudice and ignorance among the common people, whipping up the passions of the crowd, and shutting down reasoned deliberation. Demagogues overturn established customs of political conduct or promise or threaten to do so. Sadly, this is a clear description of Donald J. Trump.

As a thought experiment, ask yourself: If I weighed 900 pounds and I told you how you could lose weight over and over again and I did it louder and louder each time, would you believe me? You would probably be more inclined to do so if I had lost 500 of those pounds. If I were still 900 pounds you would probably be less inclined to believe me—no matter the conviction with which I spoke?

There's a glaring similarity between the aforementioned thought experiment and the reality of Donald Trump's father gifting him in the neighborhood of a half-billion dollars and him having to file for bankruptcy four times because he is a self-proclaimed "great deal maker." Most people have heard of his bankruptcy filings due to his failed attempt to operate casinos in Jersey City, NJ, but did you know that this "great deal maker" also failed as a professional sports team owner? In 1985, the USFL voted to move from a spring to a fall schedule in 1986 to compete directly with the NFL. This was done at the urging of New Jersey Generals majority owner Donald Trump and a handful of other owners as a way to force a merger between the leagues. As part of this strategy, the USFL filed an anti-trust lawsuit against the National Football League in 1986, and a jury ruled that the NFL had violated anti-monopoly laws. However, in a victory in name only, the USFL was awarded a judgment of just $1, which—under anti-trust laws—was tripled to $3. This court decision effectively ended the USFL's existence. The league never played the 1986 season, and by the time it folded, it had lost over 163 million U.S. dollars.

In 1988, Trump borrowed money to start Trump Airlines, and it launched on June 8, 1989. Two years later, he defaulted on the loan and the business failed. In 2007, he started *Trump Magazine*; it folded by 2009. Trump University and Trump Mortgage are among others of his failed businesses. Really, does this sound like someone who can successfully run the greatest country in the world? Unfortunately, we know the answer to that now. The point here is that Donald Trump should not have been elected solely on his proclamation of being a great deal maker, rather he should have been outright rejected based on his very public ineptitude. The fact is: Donald Trump is a skilled demagogue and nothing else. If you are a Trump supporter and you are not an elitist and you are still waiting to feel the positive impact of the Trump Presidency in your household, then it's time for you to acknowledge that you voted against your own best interest. Moreover, if you did not participate in the electoral process, then you should be ashamed of yourself because you did as much to elect Donald Trump as those who voted for him.

Irrespective of the group you find yourself associated with today, it is incumbent upon each of us to fully exercise our right to vote. That means voting in every election on every level (local municipalities and counties, state, and Federal). If you don't like a local judge, don't complain about him/her; vote for someone who is running against him/her. If you don't like your representation on the city level, vote for a different mayoral candidate and make sure that those who share your concerns go with you to vote. Are you getting a clearer picture of how this all works? Also, engaging in civil dialogue with friends and associates who share opposing views to yours is a constructive exercise, e.g., if a Facebook or Twitter friend posts how you should respect Trump as the President of all Americans, you can respond that you're sure that they showed that same fervor for the office when President Obama was in office, LOL. In all seriousness, it is a perfect opportunity to educate by espousing only the facts of the issue at hand. Just because we live in disparate districts does not mean that we should be treated differently and that we cannot participate in the process and argue for equitable treatment. Become an advocate for informed participation and not for suspending common sense. The assiduities of the entire underserved communities are essential to the fostering of equal treatment.

~~~

A FINANCIAL DECISION

Cities have to make financial decision to manage their annual budgets. One such decision involves yellow-colored street lighting for what I refer to as the yellow light districts or the economically disadvantaged neighborhoods. Although black and brown people predominantly comprise these disadvantaged neighborhoods, there are also a substantial number of disadvantaged white people in disadvantaged neighborhoods.

Yellow colored streetlights are more common than white lights in poor neighborhoods because the technology behind it is more economically viable for major cities around the country. Basically, less efficient, but cheaper technology is more prevalent in poor neighborhoods. However, it is also factual that LED technology emitting white light is on the onset of taking over the future majority, but its initial high cost is still a major impact. The question for us as taxpayers is: Why are there no white lights in the economically disadvantaged neighborhoods in any major city in America? Better yet, why are there no remaining yellow lights in the affluent neighborhoods? Both questions are easily answered. The obvious and more difficult question is: What can we do to change that unfortunate dynamic? Perhaps the answer is less difficult; it's the same as previously discussed: voting in every election and participating in city council meetings. They are our best opportunities to effectuate change, and it's the reoccurring theme throughout this book. Until we fully participate, we will continue getting the short end of the budgetary stick.

Less clear visibility is the obvious problem presented by yellow lighting. The less obvious problem has to do with what happens in the many shadows created by yellow lighting. There have been studies that yielded contrasting findings and that have led many to conclude that the illumination level is not a factor in nighttime criminal activity. Analysis of four high-crime areas in the District of Columbia found a marked reduction in crime following re-lighting (Hartley 1974). Similarly, in Kansas City, a major re-lighting program led to lower levels of robbery and assault, some of which appeared to be totally displaced (Wright et al. 1974). Contrastingly, a study in New Orleans showed negligible change in the level of night-time crime. I would posit that the New Orleans study is the exception rather than the rule. Nevertheless, assessments of sociological impact have been more encouraging and consistent, and they suggest that increased, or more uniform, lighting does reduce fear.

The streetlight illumination debate is not a recent phenomenon. Researchers and criminologists have long come down on both sides of this debate. Some criminologists have even suggested that increased illumination makes it easier for potential thieves looking for contents in parked cars. My retort to such an ignoramus is that we should put yellow lights in the affluent neighborhoods to better protect them and the contents of their cars at night. Those who are in the camp of "brighter does not mean safer" all live in the white (brighter) light districts. There is a clear cognitive dissonance in how they speak of what they believe to be true and what their actions show that they actually believe. Furthermore, it is clearly a case of using statistics to say what you want them to say. I've lived in the yellow light district, and I am fortunate enough now to live in the white light district, and I can assure you that it makes a difference on many levels. That is why police departments recommend that we leave the porch lights (front and back) on at night. According to the police, burglars prefer to work in the dark. I would posit that we could go into any major city in the country and if we invert the household occupants in the yellow and white light districts, and invert their life chances, and nothing else, that the criminal statistical data would not noticeable change. Derivatively, high-illuminating white lights are, by every measure, better than low-illuminating yellow lights on many levels. Anyone who thinks otherwise has his/her head buried in the sand or is afflicted with rectal cranial inversion (a euphemism for much harsher language). A more comprehensive understanding of the impetus of political decision-making is a requisite for enacting the desired outcome. We can only confirm the efficacy of our participation through participation.

Chapter Two
Economic and Disease Determinants

There are many factors associated with having disparate districts in American society, but make no mistake about it, they are all politically motivated. There are political and economic determinants of disease etiology/causation and treatment. Economic determinism is defined as the doctrine that all social, cultural, political, and intellectual forms are determined by or result from such economic factors as the quality of natural resources, productive capability, technological development, or the distribution of wealth. What is at play here is the distribution of wealth. A redistribution of wealth is not an advocation of robbing the rich and giving to the poor like Robin Hood. Rather, it is an advocacy for a level and fair playing field. It is a political argument to be played out by our two-party political system.

The aforementioned economic determinants are politically designed to marginalize those in the yellow light districts. A marginalized community is a group that's confined to the lower or peripheral edge of the society. The group is denied involvement in mainstream economic, political, cultural, and social activities and placed in a powerless or unimportant position within a society or group. Such alienation or disenfranchisement resulting from social exclusion is overtly connected to a person's social class, race, skin color, religious affiliation, ethnic origin, educational status, childhood relationships, living standards, or appearance. We must protest all policies meant to marginalize our community.

Similarly, according to the Centers for Disease Control and Prevention (CDC), sixty percent of premature deaths are associated with social, environmental, and behavioral circumstances. Only ten percent are the result of in-adequate clinical care, and twenty to thirty percent stem from genetics.

Additionally, the Kaiser Family Foundation found that more than one-third of total deaths in the United States every year are attributed to social factors such as low education, racial segregation, lack of social supports, and poverty. We should be responding by delivering an unprecedented, relation-ship-based, whole-person model of care that goes beyond the doctor's office, a strategy that fully integrates the social and clinical programs that produce a positive difference in our health outcomes for all Americans and not just those in the white light districts.

By ensuring that our holistic America has the critical support and services it needs, we can help the yellow light (the underserved) districts make impor-tant lifestyle changes and lead healthier, more productive lives. Obviously, I agree with the Kaiser Family Foundation, but I remind you that it requires our full participation on every level.

<center>~~~</center>

PARTY AFFILIATION

Party affiliation, especially matters involving economic and social deter-minants, should be of utmost importance to all who feel like government is not working for them personally. You should seek the understanding of which party supports more of what you believe and thus decide to which party you truly belong. Hence, let's do a simple thought experiment. By definition, a thought experiment considers a hypothesis, theory, or principle for the purpose of thinking through its consequences. Republicans are strictly against union-ization. They dismantle every union within their reach. So, is the Republican Party responsible for your economic status as an employee at a unionized com-pany? If it is, it can't; if it isn't, it must. Such a Republican can't exist. Many in the so-called middle class are registered Republicans, but the middle class was built on the backs of unions. The middle class has diminished to a mere ten percent of all jobs in the U.S. today. It is also noteworthy that no unions jobs at union facilities were the beneficiaries of higher wages because of the pres-ence of the unions. By derivation, when you give allegiance to Republicans

8

because you enjoy a higher economic status through your associations with unionization; you have misplaced allegiance and are voting against your own best interest.

Generally speaking, Democrats are socially and fiscally liberal or progressive, but there are subtle differences in the two noted terms. Pundits often use the words liberal and progressive interchangeably, but those two words are not synonymous. They do not mean the same thing, and thus should not be used as descriptions for the same thing. The word liberal usually describes two lines of thinking in modern politics in the United States. People oftentimes describe themselves as "social liberals", i.e., "socially liberal, but fiscally conservative." Those making such a claim are Republicans, rather than Democrats. Such claims by Republicans really, really strain credulity. For example, Republicans often use the liberal label when it benefits their argument, but they don't believe it themselves. They are only truly liberal when it comes to gun control or the Second Amendment. They are certainly not liberal when it comes to Roe v. Wade, or Brown v. Board of Education, or Dred Scott v. Sanford— some of the most despicable Supreme Court cases about liberties in American history. I dare they profess to be liberal when it is politically expedient. Real social liberals are Democrats who believe in balancing liberty with social justice. They tend to support gay marriage, legalizing marijuana, criminal justice reform, protecting the environment, and eliminating inequities. They allow certain liberties to be sacrificed, or balanced (like not allowing landlords to refuse someone based on their race), in lieu of discrimination. Alternatively, liberal can also be used (usually negatively) to describe someone who believes that the government can and should use tax dollars to play an active role in improving communities and promoting the general welfare of the country. In short, they believe the government should collect taxes and spend them to improve communities. While I generally ascribe to both principles, neither describes accurately what it means to be a progressive.

Progressives recognize problems and try to define and address the systemic rules, laws, and traditions that enable and empower the problems in the first place. Issues like climate change, social justice, and income inequality are pervasive topics among progressives. However, their clear and most important issue is money in politics. Because money in politics is so influential on our candidates and elected officials, progressives collectively recognize that our broken campaign finance system affects all issues. Literally, almost no issue goes unaffected by money in politics. Private prisons, gun control, education funding, the climate crisis, deregulation, health care, the over-prescription of pain killers, Supreme Court Justice appointments, etc. Our campaign finance system as presently constructed is absolutely corrupt, and while liberals would espouse those sentiments, progressive would agree but would also want to investigate what makes it corrupt. By derivation, the basic difference in liberalism and progressivism is that progressivism want to address cause and effect of a particular issue. Moreover, both liberals and progressives sanction the utilitarian ideal of government: That the morally correct course of action is the one that produces benefit for the greatest number of people in society. Hence, Democratic policies tend to be utilitarian. Evidenced by their left-shifting positions of the last thirty years, Democrats are more insistent than ever that government must play a larger role in assisting the underserved communities and in addressing the human impact of social determinants. Our broken healthcare system is but one example of this human impact of social determinants. Several factors relating to health outcomes are at play, and all of those factors are influenced by social circumstances. Social determinants of health such as poverty, unequal access to healthcare, lack of education, stigma, and racism are underlying contributing factors to health inequities. Democrats are targeting ways to address these factors that are at the root of the negative human impact of such social determinants. I would posit that incremental politics has long been the accepted normative behavior of the Democratic party. My personal feeling is that poor people will never see noticeable economic progress with incremental politics. When discrepancies between norm-driven behavior and private feelings arise, pluralistic ignorance is the result.

In social psychology, pluralistic ignorance is a situation in which a majority of group members privately reject a norm but go along with it because they assume, incorrectly, that most others accept it. Hence, I was once pluralistically ignorant because I have always believed that Democratic elected officials' normative behavior was to engage in incremental politics. Those were my private feelings that I wrongly assumed were not the feelings of a majority of Democrats. This was borne out by the followings of both Bernie Sanders and Elizabeth Warren. The clear majority of Democrats support the more progressive positions of Senators Sanders and Warren. We must continue to reject the norms promoted by those who control the narrative (the wealthy) and fight for a more equitable share in American prosperity.

Furthermore, the Democratic establishment and its punditocracy create an environment that births pluralistic ignorance. One such example involves the acceptance of a balanced budget as normative behavior. Republicans do not, for one minute, accept that notion when they are in power, but they promote it when they are not in power. The Reagan tax bill, the Bush '43 tax bill, and now the Trump tax bill are absolute proof of that proclamation.

In fact, many mainstream economists don't believe that the U.S. government debt requires urgent attention in the form of a balanced budget. A minority of economists are gaining attention with the argument that it doesn't matter whether a government that prints its own money balances its budget. The more mainstream view among economists is that the nation's debt may ultimately become a problem, but it's not one we need to face by balancing the budget right now. They cite current conditions, including historically low interest rates, which indicate that investors don't see the debt as much of a problem either. U.S. government bonds are still considered the safest investments on Earth, and decades of predictions of bond-market doom have yet to be realized.

One reason economists caution against taking drastic measures to balance the budget is the impact it would have on the economy. Balancing the budget would require steep spending cuts and tax increases which would amount to a double body blow to the U.S. economy. This could actually increase the deficit by lowering tax revenue and causing the government to spend more on social programs. The afore-documented tax cuts by Republican administrations are more than suggestive that they are in this same camp as the many mainstream economists we are citing. Furthermore, that they are truly concerned about balancing the budget when Democrats are in power strains credulity.

Another view of government deficits and debt that has risen to prominence in recent years is that of Modern Monetary Theory (MMT). Proponents of MMT, usually liberal economists and politicians, argue that deficits and debts generally don't matter because the government, unlike a household, can simply print more money. The caveat is that this theory only holds when inflation is weak or at least contained. Government borrowing becomes a problem only when it raises aggregate demand to inflationary levels, according to MMT proponents. Therefore, because a government is able to print money and raise taxes, its budget should not be compared to a household budget.

~~~

DEMAND-PULL INFLATION

There are several types of inflation, but just looking at demand-pull inflation, it is clear that this type of inflation can be caused by strong consumer demand for a product or service. When there's a surge in demand for goods across an economy, prices increase, and the result is demand-pull inflation. Consumer confidence tends to be high when unemployment is low and wages are rising, which leads to more spending. Economic expansion has a direct impact on the level of consumer spending in an economy, which can lead to high demand for products and services.

As the demand for a particular good or service increases, the available supply decreases. When fewer items are available, consumers are willing to pay more to obtain the item—as outlined in the economic principle of supply and demand. The result is higher prices due to demand-pull inflation.

Companies also play a role in inflation, especially if they manufacture popular products. A company can raise prices simply because consumers are willing to pay the increased amount. Corporations also raise prices freely when the item for sale is something consumers need for everyday existence, such as oil and gas. However, it's the demand from consumers that provides the corporations with the leverage to raise prices.

~~~

WHO BENEFITS FROM INFLATION?

While consumers experience little benefit from inflation, investors can enjoy a boost if they hold assets in markets affected by inflation. For example, those who are invested in energy companies might see a rise in their stock prices if energy prices are rising. Some companies reap the rewards of inflation if they can charge more for their products as a result of a surge in demand for their goods. If the economy is performing well and housing demand is high, home-building companies can charge higher prices for selling homes. In other words, inflation can provide businesses with pricing power and increase their profit margins. If profit margins are rising, it means the prices that companies charge for their products are increasing at a faster rate than the increases in production costs.

Also, business owners can deliberately withhold supplies from the market, allowing prices to rise to a favorable level. However, companies can also be hurt by inflation if it's the result of a surge in production costs. Companies are at risk if they're unable to pass on the higher costs to consumers through higher prices. If foreign competition, for example, is unaffected by the production cost increases, their prices wouldn't need to rise. As a result, U.S. companies might have to eat the higher production costs or otherwise risk losing customers to foreign-based companies. However, I would posit that this is a product of bad trade policies. I would also posit that since Republicans are fond of saying—when they are making tons of profits due to inflation—"allow the free market to work," then they should also be willing to allow it to work when it's not in their favor, but rather in the favor of the consumers. Why is it not capitalism at its best when it is working for consumers? By derivation, it appears that the need to balance the budget is not a real thing, even in the minds of Republicans.

As a point of reiteration and as a contrasting point, the Democratic establishment and its punditocracy could be said to be pluralistically ignorant in thinking that they cannot win an election if they support Medicare for all, free college for the poor, a clean energy infrastructure package, or a huge tax increase on the top two percent of Americans and its largest corporations. I would posit that there is a clear majority of Americans who would support such a ticket and the legislation that would follow.

It is fear and, plainly and simply, bad political calculus by the Democratic establishment and its punditocracy that has motivated them to favor centrist Democratic candidates over the far-left candidates. We need not look further than what led to Trump being elected. The Republican establishment and its punditocracy did all they could to nominate any candidate not named Donald Trump until such time that they realized that their voters wanted something different. People are exhausted with the normative behavior of the political establishment. I would posit that Bernie Sanders would have easily beaten Donald Trump in the 2016 election had the Democratic establishment and its punditocracy kept their hands off the scales during the primary election and allowed our democracy to work as it was designed to work.

As for the opposition party, the vast majority of Republicans more generally classify themselves as socially and fiscally conservative. No contemporary Republican can be regarded as an avatar of concern for the poor. Conservative beliefs are speciously characterized by respect for American traditions, support for Christian values, moral absolutism, free markets, and individualism. For example, moral absolutism is an ethical view that all actions are intrinsically right or wrong. Stealing, for instance, might be considered to always be immoral, even if done for the well-being of others and even if in the end it promotes good. If they truly believe that, why then do Republicans oppose regulations designed to prevent large corporations from stealing? Why does their moral absolutism not apply to lying to the American people as a central way of doing business as politicians? Are they absolutist only when it supports their position? If you examine each of their speciously characterized beliefs, you will find them all to be untenable.

While conservatives consider individual liberty to be the fundamental trait of democracy, liberals place a greater value on equality and social justice than on social order and tradition. As I watch what conservatives do, as opposed to what they say, I am unsure of their true ideology—i.e., "rule of law". Is not the real conservative position one that is for the rule of law for the least of us, but opposes the rule of law if it tries to hold the privileged among us accountable? For example, conservatives posit that the Black Lives Matter movement has no respect for law enforcement officers when they speak out about being shot in the back by officers. Contrast that with the position that they are currently taking when Donald Trump is publicly critical of the FBI and CIA officers who are trying to hold him accountable for his actions. This is clearly evidentiary as to what Republicans actually believe; unless, of course, you can't believe your lying eyes or ears. Politicians regularly make statements that they know to be false because they rely on the ignorance of voters. I find such dishonest rhetoric to be pernicious and condescending. Nevertheless, I would like to believe that a majority of Senators loathe (hate) the President's ridiculous behavior but are loath (reluctant) to speak out against him because of their misguided political calculus.

While conservative or right-wing politics and liberal or center-left politics in the 21st century United States both assert "Christian values" as a political stance, they are decidedly different positions: Conservatives posit censorship of sexual content, especially in movies and on television; laws against induced abortion; sexual abstinence outside the marriage arrangement; abstinence as the only sex education that's taught; the promotion of intelligent design to be taught in public schools and colleges as an alternative to evolution; the enactment of laws against same-sex marriage and the acceptance of homosexuality into mainstream society; and organized school prayer in public schools. Juxtaposed, liberals favor support for a culture of empathy and compassion (seen as central to Christianity) and support for small communities' interests over the interests of large corporations and the powerful. They also posit protection of the environment; respect for diplomacy; war as a last resort only; inclusion and acceptance of immigrants and refugees; and a living wage for all workers and the right of workers to form trade unions.

Juxtapositions notwithstanding, the accumulation of wealth into the hands of a few is the most important nisus (goal) of the Republican party. Alms-deeds (helping the poor or needy) is not on the legislative radar of Republican law makers. The contemporary Republican party cannot be regarded as an avatar of concern for the poor. Conversely, Republican politicians have an avarice with respect for the top one percent and large corporations. Additionally, they are masterful at controlling the narrative. For example, they rail against welfare and contend that it's for lazy people who don't want to work. They understand that welfare has a negative connotation that makes their position easy to sell. Therefore, they avoid using the term welfare when describing giving taxpayer dollars to large corporations. The term "corporate incentives" denotes a much more positive use of taxpayer dollars. They are either both welfare, or they are both incentives. What they are not is different—except that the former is done to address a need while the latter is done out of greed. Derivatively, only by our full participation in the election of our politicians can we change this wrong-footed dynamic by those in power. As a registered Democrat, I am inclined to remind you that Democrats are a larger swath of voters than are Republicans, and therefore if Democrats turn out to vote in every election, they would win handily. That fact notwithstanding, the real fight is not between Democrats and Republicans. Granted, that is the narrative pushed by those in power so as to distract us from the real fight. The real fight is between the billionaires and large corporations who pay to control the narrative and the rest of the population that unfortunately has no lobby. Whether we are Democrats or Republicans, Independents, or anything else, together we actually have the power to stamp out the undesirables among career politician who accept money from the lobby to control the narrative and do their dirt. If they vote against their alleged positions that got them elected, it should strain our credulity to believe that they are trustworthy, and we must vote never to send them back to represent us. This is the only way we can change the behavior of politicians who over-promise and under-deliver, or who make promises that they never intended on keeping. Virtue is not confined to the Christian world, so if our politicians have no virtue then they have no utility as our representatives. If you find that your party affiliation is counterintuitive to effectuating the outcome you desire, are you open-minded enough to change parties?

Chapter Three
Social Stratification

Social stratification is where groups of people are ranked according to their access to and possession of what is most valued in society—including money, power, and prestige. Clearly, political party affiliation does not, in every epoch, speak to one's social rank in society. The economic determinists theorize that those who control the economic institution, or the system that controls the distribution of goods and services in a society, also control all other institutions in that society. Yet, workers, or the proletariat class, operate under a false consciousness. In colloquial terms, while they may realize that they have less money than the owners of the businesses for which they work, they are unaware that the entire social system is rigged against them so that owners can gain profit at the expense of the workers. Therefore, the ideas of the ruling class are in every epoch (period of time in history) the ruling ideas. By this we mean that the most powerful class in society has disproportionate control over what is taught in schools, what is widely published, what is considered good and bad in society, and even what is preached from the pulpit. For example, cynics would posit that the religious organizations are used by our government to help control the masses and on that basis, they are given their tax-free status—a legalized quid pro quo arrangement, if you will. Clearly, the dominant class can use its power to establish a dominant ideology, a set of beliefs that support the prevailing economic or political system. Class can therefore affect people's life chances, their opportunities to improve their quality of life. It begs the question: Can we fully trust the equity of our information delivery systems (news outlets, Facebook, etc.)? For example: Are the gross domestic product (GDP), stock market rate, and unemployment rate real indicators of how well most Americans are faring in the economy? The answer is of course a resounding "NO," and every American who engages in critical thought acknowledges that reality. Yet, news outlets put forth whatever information the dominant class espouses as indicators of what constitutes a strong economy for the utility of most Americans. Assessing one's own economic situation strains credulity to believe a message that reeks of cognitive dissonance. The dissonance between what we are told and what we see and feel strikes the ear harshly. In colloquial terms, if it looks and feels unprincipled, it is difficult to accept the messengers as truth-tellers. This is not to suggest that all news is meant to deceive, but rather that it requires us to be uncharacteristically ruminative (critically thinking) to get to the truth in many instances. It should not have to be that way in a democracy, but it is, and it requires the full participation in the democratic process by every American to effectuate change.

First, though, we must understand that politically there are only two classes of people in American society today. Even though America is notionally a democracy, when there is not full participation in said democracy those who do participate are not forced to play by the rules. That results in our government actually being a plutocracy. A plutocracy is but an oligarchy in which the ruling group are the wealthiest people in that society—rather that the government, as is the case in an oligarchy. That means that the top one percent of the wealthiest people rule the rest of us. After all, they have more wealth than the bottom ninety percent combined, and that gap between the uber-wealthy and everyone else has only grown wider in the past several decades. Derivatively, the rest of us, like it or not, effectively comprise the working class in American society. Please understand that a plutocracy is very different from a democracy, in which every person's vote, ostensibly, counts equally. Of course, we understand that votes don't count equally because of the electoral college, but with full participation we could force elimination of the electoral college and thus eliminate gerrymandering (redistricting). It is that simple to have our votes count equally and take back our democracy.

Let's face it, the election of Trump was a result of the electoral college due to the explicit gerrymandering of the Republican party and the consequence of the perceived legacy of decades of neglect of the working class and a des-

perate attempt to try anything different. By countenance of most, it was a co-
lossal mistake of epic proportion that resulted in the election of the most unprincipled President in our lifetime and perhaps ever. He is decidedly the most
racist, bigoted, selectively xenophobic, pernicious, and divisive President ever.
He does not comprehend that the President of The United States is the President of all of its people: the white and the wight (all human beings). A socially
stratified society would be better served with a president whose will is to coalesce the United States into a movement capable of uniting a currently deeply
polarized country.

The polarization of this country is by tactical design. The rich and powerful have always used deception to divert our attention away from the real
fight. Our most import fight is not racial, religious, gendered, or any other of
the things they promote as our struggle. Although all of these things are real
and important in their own right, they are not our most important fight. Our
first and most important battle is a class war. It is the rich and powerful against
the rest of us who make them rich and powerful. Their prestidigitatory tactics
have so confused us that we are duped into believing that reverse racism is a
real thing and in fighting in a manner that will always produce a victory for
them. Although, some folks genuinely believe reverse racism is happening to
white Americans. The reality is that, while individual prejudice and discrimination against majority groups exist, systemic reverse racism isn't exactly a
thing because an essential component of racism requires power, and in the
U.S., people of color largely lack the power to damage the interests of white
people as a whole. The idea of reverse racism stems as far back as the Reconstruction era. Following the U.S. Civil War in the 1860s, discussions about
how to proceed post-slavery created questions about black and white rights.
When discussing whether to offer former slaves reparations, some white
people were concerned that the advancement of black people would cause setbacks for them. Those in power would love to have that fight be at the fore-
front of racist dialogue. Hence, the Black Lives Matter movement and the rise
of white supremacy around President Donald Trump have fueled charges of
reverse racism in the late 2010s. The slogan All Lives Matter, a criticism of
Black Lives Matter (which focuses on police brutality against black people), is
often seen as motivated by fears of reverse racism. In 2018, a year after a white
nationalist killed a counter-protester at the Unite the Right rally in Charlottes-

ville, Virginia, Trump tweeted showing support for both sides, essentially promoting the notion of reverse racism.

Additionally, the Religious Right has been prominent in scapegoating blacks. As William Martin thoroughly documents in *With God on Our Side: The Rise of the Religious Right in America* (1996), that began with efforts to draw white Southern evangelicals into the Republican party by opposing desegregation and attacking "intrusive government regulations" like the Civil Rights Act of 1964. Decade by decade, this pattern of diversionary scapegoating continued: Opposition to racial integration gave way to equally hysterical attacks on civil rights for women, for gay people, and for the transgender. We need to resist falling into this giant trap of misinformation and deception. We must shrewdly resist any distraction that allows the rich and powerful to continue to widen the inequity gap. Furthermore, social stratification is only made worse by what is clearly a broken criminal justice system.

CRIMINAL JUSTICE REFORM

I think it's colossally inappropriate and, dare I say, egregious to characterize our system of American jurisprudence as one where "a person is considered innocent until proven guilty in a court of law." I would posit that the system treats you as if you're guilty and the burden is upon you to prove your innocence. That is part and parcel of the reason for a disproportionate number of black and brown men being deprived of their conjugal felicity or happiness. The nuclear family of black and brown men are badly positioned by the inequities of the American judiciary. The inequities abound throughout the system for all non-whites, but also for poor white people. For example, pretrial publicity that may be extremely prejudicial to a defendant's right to a fair trial is a product of media coverage before the trial begins. Most any action of the poor causes an inference of criminal intent. Conversely, there is a superficiality with which we talk about the decisions of the influential, e.g., the war on drugs and its effect on African American men. My animus for the advocacy of unintended consequence as reasoning for so many black men having been affected by the drug statute is immeasurable. Too often that which is characterized as an unintended consequence is but intellectual dishonesty. There cannot be unintended consequences where there are clear selectivity biases. But for selectivity biases, white families would have been afflicted with the single parent family epidemic that destroyed nuclear family units of so many black and brown families. The fact that the statute deems crack cocaine ("a black and brown person's drug") one-hundred times more penal than powdered cocaine ("a white person's drug") predicates intentionality. Beyond the penalty for cocaine there are many disparities in federal criminal sentencing for blacks or browns and whites. Inexplicably, black men receive a sentence ten times that of comparable white men for the same crime. While black men only make up six percent of the U.S. population, they comprise about thirty-five percent of the prison population and are incarcerated at a rate about six times that of white men. About one in three black men will be incarcerated at some point in their life. This inequity can largely be attributed to the "judicial discretion in sentencing" statute. If you are a person of color, you are most likely opposed to this statute because it has played a significant role in black and brown people being more harshly sentenced than whites for the same exact crimes. Mandatory sentencing, completely divorced from judicial discretion, would eliminate the apparent biases in sentencing. The judiciary body used to be an august body, but we should now all be aghast at the indignant behavior and prejudicial positions of any of its members. According to The Sentencing Project, the United States effectively operates two distinct criminal justice systems: one for wealthy people and another for poor people and people of color. The wealthy can access a vigorous adversary system replete with constitutional protections for defendants. The experiences of the poor and minority defendants within the criminal justice system often differ substantially from those of the wealthy due to a number of factors, each of which contributes to the overrepresentation of such individuals in the system. It is a form of racism and classism and thus prejudices the public good which makes it unlawful by statute. Reforming our broken criminal justice system requires our standing up during every voting cycle in our local communities as well as on the federal level. Attend town hall meeting when your congressional representatives return home and ask questions of them about why and how they voted on specific issues. Don't allow them to answer your questions in the abstract, but rather insist on specificity and most especially on how they voted on the statute in question. If you feel like your position is not being represented, don't allow the congresspersons to filibuster and avoid answering the questions asked of them. This is another way that we can hold our elected officials accountable.

Akin to the federal war on drugs policy are many other state and municipal policies that are intended to disproportionately affect poor people. In Texas, for example, there existed what was termed the Driver Responsibility Program that was clearly designed to trap low-income drivers in a cycle of debt. Effective September 1, 2019, the State of Texas has repealed the Driver Responsibility Program and replaced it with a $2 insurance fee for every annual auto insurance policy. Previously, under the Driver Responsibility Program, as of January 2018, 1.4 million drivers (nearly ten percent of the state's drivers that year) had suspended licenses for not paying surcharges. Over ninety percent of suspensions in 2017 were due to driving without insurance or a valid license, according to a report by the Texas Fair Defense Project, an advocacy organization that represents many people whose licenses have been suspended as part of the program. I congratulate the Senate body on finally taking action to get rid of this long-standing program which aggressively targeted poor people disproportionately. Congratulations notwithstanding, our full participation in the democratic process would have forced change years earlier. Don't despair, though; there are many more such unfair practices within every municipality across the country that still need our dogged determination and assiduity to change. Let's go to our local city council meetings and demand an explanation for why our police no longer "serve and protect," but rather "harass and collect." Our meeting participation will help us to be informed about local matters and to learn the names of the elected officials. That knowledge is our power, and the power of the people is then greater than the people in power.

Chapter Four
The Power of an Active Democracy

The power of the people can overcome the people in power. But, the people have no power if they do not fully participate and if they allow the same old bad actors to remain in power. Aristotle said: "We are what we repeatedly do." By extension, our excellence or deficiency isn't an act, it's a habit. Make it a habit of knowing the issues and candidates you are voting on or for. Rule of the majority is commonly referred to as a democracy, but it is a system of government that requires its citizens to vote in order to exercise their power. Additionally, citizens can also contact their elected officials when they want to support or change a law. According to the Declaration of Independence, the government gets its power to govern from the people that it governs. As the Declaration exclaims: "Governments are instituted among men, deriving their just powers from the consent of the governed." Our democracy needs active citizens in order to work properly. "We the people" are the first words of the Constitution and are written larger than anything else. The framers of the Constitution wanted to make it clear that the power must be of the people, not their representatives. A democracy is important because it gives citizens equal opportunities to help enact laws, vote for leaders, and be protected by laws and rights that are in place. Voting and a democracy are very important in a nation because they provide people an opportunity to voice their opinions and vote for what they believe in; it holds elected officials accountable for their behavior while in office, and it prevents a minority from dictating the policies to the majority. These things are not currently happening because we are not all fully participating in the political process.

Political participation is largely assumed as an act of taking part in political action. A participatory democracy is primarily concerned with ensuring that citizens are afforded an opportunity to participate or otherwise be involved in making decisions on matters that affect their lives. Therefore, a participatory democracy requires your full participation. Involvement on the municipal, state, and federal levels are all equally essential if we are to effectuate change in the yellow light districts. Public or citizen participation is a political principle or practice, and it may also be recognized as a right…The principle of public participation holds that those who are affected by a decision have a right to be involved in the decision-making process. The idea is to force equity in how tax dollars are allocated among districts. Municipal governments are the counties, city, town, or district and are responsible for areas such as libraries, school districts, parks, community water systems, local police, roadways, and parking.

According to American political scientist Larry Diamond, a democracy has three key elements: a political system for choosing and replacing the government officials through free and fair elections; the active and full participation of the people, as citizens, in politics and in civic life; and the protection of the human rights of all citizens. It is incumbent upon the citizenry to ensure that those four elements are respected and remain intact. We must refuse to allow our democracy to be rigged by elected officials. Let's examine each element separately.

First, choosing and replacing officials through free and fair elections. Free means that all those entitled to vote have the right to be registered and to vote and must be free to make their choice without fear of intimidation. Free also means that unnecessary expenses beyond registration and any simple form of identify are not necessary. Any requirement beyond what is necessary to join the military, get a driver's license or state ID, or matriculate at a college or university is an attempt to disenfranchise a specific portion of the electorate. If our local officials are trying, in any way, to make it difficult for us to vote or do not take a public stand against those who are, we must be determined not to re-elect them to office. With respects to fair, a fair election is one in which all voters have an equal opportunity to register, where all votes are counted, and where the announced results reflect the actual vote totals. In a presidential election, "fair" has a more complex meaning due to the electoral college. The party in power has the lawful right to redraw the districts so that it unfairly benefits their party. It is time that we take away party officials' ability to ger-rymander districts no matter our party affiliation. First, we must understand that we are not in a racial fight, but rather a class struggle. Those in power—placed there by the wealthiest and most powerful among us—use race, eth-nicity, and religious affiliation to their advantage. Dr. King's definition of racism was "prejudice plus power." Black people might certainly be capable of prejudice, but they are lacking any real power, so one is hard-pressed to ad-vance the claim of reverse racism; to suggest such a thing would be a false equivalency. Many of us have heard prejudice in our heads and felt it in our hearts. But prejudicial preconception is not the same as having the power to put prejudice into practice.

～

AMERICAN CAPITALISM

"This is a capitalist society" is the familiar retort that seems to get repeated to anyone who questions why the American economic system is so exploitative. When Americans declare that "we live in a capitalist society" they are simply arguing against being regulated. According to the Organization for Eco-nomic Cooperation and Development (O.E.C.D.), in the United States, the richest one percent of Americans own forty percent of the country's wealth, while a larger share of working-age people live in poverty. In a capitalist so-ciety, wages are depressed as businesses compete over the price—not the quality—of goods; so-called unskilled workers are typically incentivized through punishments, not promotions; inequality reigns and poverty spreads. Additionally, while other capitalistic societies have as much as ninety percent of their workforce unionized, only ten percent of American wage and salaried workers carry union cards because our Republican lawmakers have long worked to destroy unions in this country. It speaks to the brutality of Amer-ican capitalism that has a long and storied history as far back as slavery in the south. As chronicled by the 1619 Project: Those searching for reasons the American economy is uniquely severe and unbridled have found answers in many places (religion, politics, culture). But recently, historians have pointed persuasively to the gnatty fields of Georgia and Alabama, to the cotton houses and slave auction blocks, as the birthplace of America's low-road approach to capitalism. Slavery was undeniably a font of phenomenal wealth. By the eve of the Civil War, the Mississippi Valley was home to more millionaires per capita than anywhere else in the United States. Cotton grown and picked by enslaved workers was the nation's most valuable export. The combined value of enslaved people exceeded that of all the railroads and factories in the nation. New Orleans boasted a denser concentration of banking capital than New York City. What made the cotton economy boom in the United States, and not in all the other far-flung parts of the world with climates and soil suitable to the crop, was our nation's unflinching willingness to use violence on nonwhite people and to exert its will on seemingly endless supplies of land and labor. Given the choice between modernity and barbarism, prosperity and poverty, lawfulness and cruelty, democracy and totalitarianism, America chose all of the above. Nearly two average American lifetimes (seventy-nine years) have passed since the end of slavery—only two. It is not surprising that we can still feel the looming presence of this institution which helped turn a poor, fledgling nation into a financial colossus.

According to dictionary.com, capitalism is an economic and political system in which property, business, and industry are owned by private individuals and not by the state. I would posit that American capitalism is in reality crony capitalism: This is a term describing an economy in which success in business depends on close relationships between business people and government, or a situation whereby those in power in government confer special benefits, or government contracts, to friends and donors after bypassing official processes like competitive bidding and the will of the people. Campaigns financed by big corporations and wealthy and powerful individuals have permeated American politics as far back as slavery, and the tactic persists to this day. These are problems that are solvable through our earnest participation in the political process. This can become a watershed moment in political history whereby we as a people take back our republic. It will not be easy, as there is so much change required to reform the system back to its original design of our forefathers.

~

Understanding The Filibuster

Among the things we must address is the filibuster. The filibuster was initially conceived of as a way to ensure that minority opinions were heard and understood before the Senate voted on an issue. Senate rules first allowed for filibusters in 1806, though the first filibuster actually occurred more than thirty years later, in 1837. They continued to be rare for more than another century.

The idea behind the filibuster was simple: As long as a senator kept talking on the floor, a bill could not move forward. Throughout the 19th century, the Senate left ending the filibuster up to the filibustering senators. When they felt they had been adequately heard, they could give up the floor and allow debate to move on to a vote.

In 1917, at the behest of President Wilson, the Senate adopted a procedure known as the cloture vote, which could end a filibuster. If a cloture vote is called for, a super-majority of senators can force an end to debate and bring the question under consideration to an up or down vote. Initially, achieving cloture required a vote from two thirds of all elected senators; the number was later changed to three fifths of all elected senators. For the next sixty years, the filibuster continued to be used sparingly.

In 1975, though, the Senate made a change that made it significantly easier to filibuster by adopting rules that allow other business to be conducted while a filibuster is technically underway. Since that time, senators have not needed to stand up on the floor and make their case to their colleagues and their constituents in order to halt legislation. Instead, these "virtual filibusters" can be conducted in absentia (in absence of the person involved). We must demand that the 1975 change to the filibuster is repealed.

~

Use Of The Filibuster

The filibuster has been used 1,300 times since 1917. However, the vast majority of those filibusters have taken place in recent years. Filibuster use began to increase dramatically in the 1970s. Even so, there still had only been a grand total of 413 Senate filibusters by 1990. Over the last twelve years, however, the filibuster was used nearly six hundred times! These filibusters aren't just being used to extend debates or stall votes; today, senators filibuster motions to proceed, preventing bills from being debated at all. A device intended to promote comprehensive discussion has turned into a tool to keep ideas from even being heard. This charade cannot stand. We must be insistent that the people's work is carried out in a reasonable and timely manner.

～

Effects Of The Filibuster

Even with the 1975 rules change allowing the Senate to conduct other business while a filibuster is underway, every filibuster kicks off a complex set of Senate procedures that can bring the Senate to a halt for up to a week and prevent other critical issues from being addressed. Filibusters on motions to proceed prevent the Senate from even being able to consider ideas for how to solve our country's big problems. For years now, small numbers of senators representing a very small percentage of the country have kept the Senate from even discussing important legislation that has passed committee review.

Additionally, virtual filibusters allow small numbers of senators to effortlessly place personal political agendas above the work of government—with no consequence. As a result, even routine Senate functions like approving executive appointees get mired in partisan politics, resulting in many vacancies on federal judiciary benches. Major pieces of legislation, including a bill that would have provided medical care for 9/11 responders, have enjoyed majority support in the Senate, yet died in the face of filibusters for lack of cloture. Legislation that should pass into law has been canceled and courts have been thrown into disarray, but the senators who have helped make that happen have never needed to actually make a case to their colleagues or their constituents. These points were originally expressed by Rick Barry and spurred me to thinking about what we need to do about the filibuster. I conclude that we must insist upon the removal of the filibuster so that legislation can move forward based on a simple up or down vote whereby constituents can see how their representatives voted.

Lest we forget, filibusters were particularly useful to southern senators who sought to block civil rights legislation, including anti-lynching legislation, until cloture (a method of closing a debate and causing an immediate vote to be taken on the question) was invoked after a sixty-day filibuster against the Civil Rights Act of 1964. In 1975, the Senate reduced the number of votes required for cloture from two-thirds to three-fifths, or sixty of the current one hundred senators. Similarly, South Carolina's J. Strom Thurmond filibustered for twenty-four hours and eighteen minutes against the Civil Rights Act of 1957. These are two of the most despicable uses of the filibuster imaginable.

Juxtaposed, Senator Huey P. Long effectively used the filibuster against bills that he thought favored the rich over the poor. The Louisiana Senator once held the Senate floor for fifteen hours. Although it was for a good cause, a simple up or down vote is sufficient enough for us to hold our representatives accountable. Let me reiterate: We must be insistent that the people's work is carried out in a reasonable and timely manner. The filibuster, in every epoch, has prevented the expedition of legislation.

~~~

SIMPLE MAJORITY VOTING

Although not explicitly mandated, the Constitution and its framers clearly envisioned that simple majority voting would be used to conduct business. The Constitution provides, for example, that a majority of each House constitutes a quorum (the minimum number of an assembly that must be present at any of its meetings to make the proceedings of that meeting valid) to do business. Meanwhile, a small number of super-majority requirements were explicitly included in the original document, including conviction on impeachment charges (two-thirds of Senate), expelling a member of Congress (two-thirds of the chamber in question), overriding presidential vetoes (two-thirds of both Houses), ratifying treaties (two-thirds of Senate), and proposing constitutional amendments (two-thirds of both Houses). Through negative textual implication, the Constitution also gives a simple majority the power to set procedural rules: "Each House may determine the Rules of its Proceedings, punish its Members for disorderly behavior, and, with the Concurrence of two thirds, expel a Member."

Commentaries in *The Federalist Papers* confirm this understanding. In "Federalist No. 58," the Constitution's primary drafter James Madison defended the document against routine super-majority requirements, either for a quorum or a "decision":

It has been said that more than a majority ought to have been required for a quorum; and in particular cases, if not in all, more than a majority of a quorum for a decision. That some advantages might have resulted from such a precaution, cannot be denied. It might have been an additional shield to some particular interests, and another obstacle generally to hasty and partial measures. But these considerations are outweighed by the inconveniences in the opposite scale.

In all cases where justice or the general good might require new laws to be passed, or active measures to be pursued, the fundamental principle of free government would be reversed. It would be no longer the majority that would rule: the power would be transferred to the minority. Were the defensive privilege limited to particular cases, an interested minority might take advantage of it to screen themselves from equitable sacrifices to the general weal, or, in particular emergencies, to extort unreasonable indulgences.

In "Federalist No. 22," Alexander Hamilton described super-majority requirements as being one of the main problems with the previous Articles of Confederation, and identified several evils which would result from such a requirement:

To give a minority a negative upon the majority (which is always the case where more than a majority is requisite to a decision), is, in its tendency, to subject the sense of the greater number to that of the lesser.

The necessity of unanimity in public bodies, or of something approaching towards it, has been founded upon a supposition that it would contribute to security. But its real operation is to embarrass the administration, to destroy the energy of the government, and to substitute the pleasure, caprice, or artifices of an insignificant, turbulent, or corrupt junto, to the regular deliberations and decisions of a respectable majority. In those emergencies of a nation, in which the goodness or badness, the weakness or strength of its government, is of the greatest importance, there is commonly a necessity for action. The public business must, in some way or other, go forward. If a pertinacious minority can control the opinion of a majority, respecting the best mode of conducting it, the majority, in order that something may be done, must conform to the views of the minority; and thus the sense of the smaller number will overrule that of the greater, and give a tone to the national proceedings. Hence, tedious delays; continual negotiation and intrigue; contemptible compromises of the public good. And yet, in such a system, it is even happy when such compromises can take place: for upon some occasions things will not admit of accommodation; and then the measures of government must be injuriously suspended, or fatally defeated. It is often, by the impracticability of obtaining the concurrence of the necessary number of votes, kept in a state of inaction. Its situation must always savor of weakness, sometimes border upon anarchy.

By derivation, the sixty-vote supermajority essentially allows the minority to control the majority. By every reasonable measure, that is not representative of a true democracy where one vote for a one-person majority is supposed to have the final say.

However, the modern-era filibuster and the effective sixty-vote super-majority requirement it has led to have had significant policy and political effects on all three branches of the federal government…

…Congress:

The supermajority rule has made it very difficult, often impossible, for Congress to pass any but the most non-controversial legislation in recent decades. During times of unified party control, majorities have attempted (with varying levels of success) to enact their major policy priorities through the budget reconciliation process, resulting in legislation constrained by budget rules. Meanwhile, public approval for Congress as an institution has fallen to its lowest levels ever, with large segments of the public seeing the institution as ineffective. Shifting majorities of both parties—and their supporters—have often been frustrated as major policy priorities articulated in political campaigns are unable to obtain passage following an election.

…Presidency:

Presidents of both parties have increasingly filled the policymaking vacuum with expanded use of executive power, including executive orders in areas that had traditionally been handled through legislation. For example, Barack Obama effected major changes in immigration policy by issuing work permits to some undocumented workers, while Donald Trump has issued several significant executive orders since taking office in 2017, along with undoing many of Obama's initiatives. As a result, policy in these areas is increasingly determined by executive preference, and is more easily changed after elections, rather than through more permanent legislative policy. Had the Affordable Care Act been passed by a simple majority, Donald Trump would not have been able to reverse it through executive order. Similarly, the next Democratic President can undo any Trump executive order. Derivatively, simple majority legislation and policies are more permanent—as our forefathers originally intended.

...Judiciary:

The Supreme Court's caseload has declined significantly, with various commenters suggesting that the decline in major legislation has been a major cause. Meanwhile, more policy issues are resolved judicially without action by Congress—despite the existence of potential simple majority support in the Senate—on topics such as the legalization of same-sex marriage. While Congress has long been an august body sent to represent constituents of the states and territories, we should all be aghast at their ineffectiveness in legislating. They are, by any measure, derelict in their duties which they were elected to perform. They continually relinquish more of their inherent responsibilities to the Executive and Judiciary branches. I am personally inclined to suggest that we rid ourselves of the dysfunctional legislative branch (Congress) because they are asleep at the wheel. However, the more reasonable course of action is that we insist on moving back in the direction of the framers of our Constitution. First, we must stop electing and reelecting do-nothing politicians. We may mistakenly elect them for one term, but there is no excuse for reelecting them. We must be absolutely insistent on electing real public servants. Then we must insist that they remove the filibuster and return to the more functional simple majority vote. These two things, combined with our refusal to accept Delphic responses to our concerns, represent a monumental first step that is essential to restoring and keeping our Republic.

～～～

Campaign Finance Reform

Additionally, the role that campaign contributions play in elections has long been a subject of debate, and that debate has increased in recent decades. Campaign finance, organization, and strategy affect which candidates get selected, the policies they promote, and who wins elections. Therefore, the role of money in campaigns remains a contentious issue, particularly whether Congress should regulate who can contribute money to campaigns, and how much money they should be allowed to contribute.

The decision in Citizens United held that political spending by corporations, associations, and labor unions is a form of free speech and therefore protected under the First Amendment. The Supreme Court's ruling in Citizens United and similar cases have reduced the limits on campaign contributions, encouraged the creation of super PACs, and increased debate over the role money can and should play in elections.

However, we are not naive to the facts. We know that political parties and candidates require money to publicize their electoral platforms and to pursue effective campaigns. We also understand that attempts to regulate campaign finance reflect the commonly held belief that uncontrolled political fundraising and spending can undermine the integrity of the democratic process and erode the confidence of the electorate in political institutions.

Consider this simple, straight-forward approach, though. It is certainly true that political parties and candidates require money to publicize their electoral platforms and to pursue effective campaigns. However, it is not necessary that political candidates receive money that can be used for their personal enrichment after they are in elected office. That is the textbook definition of quid pro quo—if you provide funds for me to get me elected, then I will do something for you once I am in office—and it must not be permitted. The elected official might very well do something for the donor because they genuinely have a shared position. But there must be legislation that prohibits elected officials from being paid by a campaign donor once they are in elected office, shared position or not. Violators must be removed from Congress if proven to be guilty of violating said legislation. This seems an impossible task because most of our politicians receive money from some of their supporters while in elected office. I can assure you that it is impossible if we don't make it one of our priorities to stop it. There are politicians honest enough to put forth such legislation that makes this illegal. Once that legislation is introduced, we must make note of those representatives that vote against the legislation, and in so doing we will have taken a huge step in identifying those who are serving for self-aggrandizement or enrichment. At that point we should realize that we must not vote to re-elect those individuals. WE CAN DO THIS!

Chapter Five
The American Experiment

The American experiment was unique and improbable in 1776, when Thomas Jefferson penned the Declaration of Independence and the American colonies defied Britain, the most powerful nation on earth at the time. As we look around the world at how difficult it is for democracy and freedom to take hold and flourish, America seems like a political miracle.

In 1787, when the Founding Fathers had hammered out the U.S. Constitution in Independence Hall in Philadelphia, Benjamin Franklin told an inquiring woman what the gathering had produced, "A republic, madam, if you can keep it." Jefferson also knew how great the American experiment's appeal would be to others. "The flames kindled on the 4th of July, 1776, have spread across too much of the globe to be extinguished by the feeble engines of despotism; on the contrary, they will consume the engines and all who work them." The self-evident truth that "all men are created equal; endowed by their creator with the right to life, liberty and the pursuit of happiness" remains the powerful philosophical and moral foundation of a successful foreign policy no less than it is the foundation of the American republic itself. Yet, as we are seeing today, the advance of freedom and democracy is not a straight path, but one that also sustains setbacks. Americans have kept their republic and built it to be strong, but it will only remain so under constant vigilance.

According to a Pew Research Center poll released earlier on global views of America: Public rejection of American democracy is prevalent in most countries. This may reflect opinions about the way in which the United States has implemented its pro-democracy agenda, and also about America's democratic values themselves. In forty-three of forty-seven countries surveyed, a majority say that the United States promotes democracy mostly where it serves its interests, rather than as a matter of principle. Even more unfortunately, this cynicism also includes sixty-three percent in the United States itself. Only forty-five percent of Americans have faith in American leadership in the world.

How to restore faith in the American political system and in its importance as a model for democracy to be exported and shared will, for the most part, be the job of the next President of the United States. Clearly, Donald J. Trump is not equipped with anything close to what it takes even to understand what a democracy is supposed to be about.

Chapter Six
Redistricting and Gerrymandering

Gerrymandering is when a political group tries to change a voting district to create a result that helps them or hurts the group who is against them. Gerrymandering works by wasting votes. It puts more votes of winners into the district they will win so the losers win in another district. While it is but one example of how gerrymandering can have a significant effect on election outcomes, this kind of disproportional representation of the public seems to be problematic for the legitimacy of democratic systems, regardless of one's political affiliation. Furthermore, honest political brokers would work tirelessly to make gerrymandering illegal.

"The Gerrymander" first appeared in a cartoon map in the *Boston Gazette*, March 26, 1812. Another definition of gerrymandering is the practice of setting boundaries of electoral districts to favor specific political interests within legislative bodies, often resulting in districts with convoluted, winding boundaries rather than compact areas. Gerrymandering in the United States has been long used to increase the power of a political party; the term "gerrymandering" was coined on review of Massachusetts's redistricting maps of 1812 set by Governor Eldridge Gerry, and the term was so named for the district's resemblance to a salamander. However, there isn't a salamander that was ever born that could twist its body to resemble the district boundaries drawn today. Boundaries are drawn with any configuration necessary to disadvantage the other group.

In the United States, redistricting takes place in each state about every ten years, following the decennial census. This defines geographical boundaries, with each district within a state being geographically contiguous and having about the same number of state voters. The resulting map affects the elections of the state's members of the United States House of Representatives and the state legislative bodies. Redistricting has always been regarded as a political exercise, which in most states is controlled by state legislators and the governor. When one party controls the state's legislative bodies and governor's office, it is in a strong position to gerrymander district boundaries to the advantage of their side and the disadvantage of their political opponents. Since 2010, detailed maps and high-speed computing have facilitated gerrymandering by political parties in the redistricting process, in order to gain control of state legislation and congressional representation, and to potentially maintain that control over several decades even against shifting political changes in a state's population.

Typical gerrymandering cases in the United States take the form of partisan gerrymandering, where the redistricting is aimed to favor one political party or weaken another, bipartisan gerrymandering that is used to protect incumbents by multiple political parties, and racial gerrymandering, aimed to weaken the power of minority voters.

Through the 20th century and since then, the U.S. court system has deemed extreme cases of gerrymandering to be unconstitutional but has struggled with how to define the types of gerrymandering and standards to be used to determine when redistricting maps are unconstitutional. The Supreme Court of the United States has affirmed in Miller v. Johnson (1995) that racial gerrymandering is a violation of constitutional rights and upheld decisions against redistricting purposely devised based on race. However, the Supreme Court has struggled as to when partisan gerrymandering occurs, e.g., Vieth v. Jubelirer (2004) and Gill v. Whitford (2018). And in a landmark decision in 2019 in Rucho v. Common Cause, the Supreme Court ultimately decided that questions of partisan gerrymandering represent a nonjusticiable political question that cannot be dealt with by the federal court system. This decision leaves it to states and Congress to develop remedies to challenge and prevent partisan gerrymandering. Some states have created independent redistricting commissions to reduce political drivers for redistricting.

Redistricting plans can be gerrymandered to dilute votes cast by minorities by a process referred to as "packing," whereby a high numbers of minority voters are packed into a small number of districts or through another process referred to as "cracking," referring to cracking minority groups by placing small numbers of minority voters into a large number of districts.

The majority opinion stated that extreme partisan gerrymandering is still unconstitutional, but it is up to Congress and state legislative bodies to find ways to restrict that, such as through the use of independent redistricting commissions.

While the U.S. Supreme Court has ruled that redistricting that discriminates on racial or ethnic grounds is unconstitutional, it has been reluctant to issue a similarly-strong ruling for partisan redistricting. The Court has ruled that excessive partisan gerrymandering violates the Constitution. Unfortunately, this Supreme Court ruling reeks of partisanship. Surely the Court recognizes that "excessive" is relative, and therefore they really ruled in favor of partisan redistricting.

Most of the gerrymandering that people get upset about involves partisan redistricting. Much of it was done by Republicans after the 2010 Census in the last redistricting cycle. In some states, like Pennsylvania and North Carolina, Republicans were able to draw districts that gave them majorities in their statehouses and congressional delegations, despite winning only a minority of votes statewide.

The key to fixing gerrymandering is changing key statutory laws for how elections are held. We must get involved at the state and local levels in order to effectuate change to this broken redistricting and gerrymandering system.

Chapter Seven
Electoral College

The Electoral College is a body of electors established by the United States Constitution, which forms every four years for the sole purpose of electing the President and Vice President of the United States. In the American electoral college system, each state gets a certain number of electors based on its total number of representatives in Congress. Each elector casts one electoral vote following the general election; there are a total of 538 electoral votes. The candidate that gets more than half (270) wins the election.

Miller v. Johnson, 515 U.S. 900 (1995), was a United States Supreme Court case concerning "affirmative gerrymandering/racial gerrymandering," where racial minority-majority electoral districts are created during redistricting to increase minority Congressional representation. Appellees (voters in the new Eleventh District which joins metropolitan black neighborhoods together with the poor black populace of coastal areas 260 miles away) challenged the district on the grounds that it was a racial gerrymander in violation of the Equal Protection Clause as interpreted in Shaw v. Reno, 509 U.S. 630. The District Court agreed, holding that evidence of the state legislature's purpose, as well as the district's irregular borders, showed that race was the overriding and predominant force in the districting determination. The court assumed that compliance with the Act would be a compelling interest but found that the plan was not narrowly tailored to meet that interest since the Act did not require three majority-black districts. The Court held: Georgia's congressional redistricting plan violates the Equal Protection Clause, pages 910-928.

Established in Article II, Section 1 of the U.S. Constitution, the Electoral College is the formal body which elects the President and Vice President of the United States. Each state has as many "electors" in the Electoral College as it has Representatives and Senators in the United States Congress, and the District of Columbia has three electors. When voters go to the polls in a Presidential election, they actually are voting for the slate of electors vowing to cast their ballots for that ticket in the Electoral College.

Additionally, the Twenty-third Amendment, ratified in 1961, provides that the District of Columbia (D.C.) is entitled to the number of electors it would have if it were a state, but no more than the least populated state (presently 3). U.S. territories are not entitled to any electors, as they are not states.

Following the national presidential election, which takes place the Tuesday after the first Monday of November, each state counts its popular votes according to that state's laws to designate presidential electors. In the contiguous forty-eight states, the winner of the plurality of the statewide vote receives all of the electors; in Maine and Nebraska, two electors are assigned in this manner and one elector allocated based on the plurality of votes in each congressional district. Electors are typically required to pledge to vote for the winning candidate, but there is an ongoing legal dispute about whether electors are required to vote as they pledged. State electors meet in their respective state capitals the first Monday after the second Wednesday of December to cast their votes. The results are counted by Congress, where they are tabulated nationally in the first week of January before a joint meeting of the Senate and House of Representatives, presided over by the Vice President, acting as president of the Senate. If a majority of votes are not cast for a candidate, the House turns itself into a presidential election session, where one vote is assigned to each of the fifty states, excluding the District of Columbia. The elected president and vice president are inaugurated on January 20. While the electoral vote has generally given the same result as the popular vote, this has not been the case in several elections, most recently in the 2016 election.

The Electoral College system is a matter of ongoing debate. Supporters of the Electoral College argue that it is fundamental to American federalism, requires candidates to appeal to voters outside of large cities, increases the political influence of small states, preserves the two-party system, and makes the electoral outcome appear more legitimate than that of a nationwide popular vote.

Opponents of the Electoral College argue that it can result in different candidates winning the popular and electoral vote (which occurred in two of the five presidential elections from 2000 to 2016); that it causes candidates to focus their campaigning disproportionately in a few "swing states"; and that its allocation of Electoral College votes gives citizens in less populated states (e.g., Wyoming) as much as four times the voting power of citizens in more populous states (e.g., California).

Two of the nation's last three Presidents won the Presidency in the Electoral College, even though they lost the popular vote nationwide. In 2000, Al Gore outpolled George W. Bush by more than 540,000 votes but lost in the Electoral College, 271–266. Sixteen years later, Hillary Clinton tallied almost three million more votes than Donald Trump but lost decisively in the Electoral College, 306–232. And, as a recent *New York Times* poll suggested, the 2020 election could very well again deliver the presidency to the loser of the popular vote. Despite this, defenders of the Electoral College argue that it was created to combat majority tyranny and support federalism, and that it continues to serve those purposes. For example, Representative Dan Crenshaw of Texas, responding to Representative Alexandria Ocasio-Cortez's recent criticism of the Electoral College, tweeted that "we live in a republic, which means 51% of the population doesn't get to boss around the other 49%," and that the Electoral College "promotes more equal regional representation and protects the interests of sparsely populated states." But arguments like these are flawed, misunderstanding the pertinent history. Below, as outlined in letters@theatlantic.com, are five common mistakes made in arguing for the preservation of the Electoral College:

Mistake Number 1: Many supporters of the Electoral College assume that the debate about presidential selection at the Constitutional Convention, like the debate today, focused on whether the president should be chosen by the Electoral College or by a nationwide popular vote. But as tempting as it is to read history in the light of contemporary concerns, the debate at the convention focused on a different issue: Should Congress choose the president? Both the Virginia Plan and the New Jersey Plan (the two primary alternatives at the Convention) proposed that Congress select the president. This was unsurprising because in most states at the time, the legislature chose the governor. On June 1, the convention voted eight to two that Congress should elect the president, and the delegates would affirm that decision on three other occasions.

The frequency with which the delegates revisited the issue reveals not their confidence but their dissatisfaction. Most delegates wanted the executive to check legislative usurpations and block unjust or unwise laws, but they feared that dependence on the legislature for election and possible reelection would compromise the executive's independence. Some delegates hoped to avoid this danger by limiting the president to a single term, but as Governor Morris of Pennsylvania observed, this could deprive the nation of a highly qualified executive, eliminate the hope of continuation in office as a spur to good behavior, and encourage the executive to "make hay while the sun shines." James Madison added that election by the legislature would "agitate and divide the legislature so much that the public interest would materially suffer" and might invite the intervention of foreign powers seeking to influence the choice.

The difficulty lay in finding an alternative to legislative selection, and the delegates considered and rejected various possibilities, including popular election. Ultimately, perhaps in desperation, they referred the issue to the Committee on Unfinished Parts. On September 4, less than two weeks before the convention ended, the committee proposed the Electoral College. Its proposal mirrored the states' distribution of power in Congress; each state had as many electoral votes as it had members of Congress. But because the electors dispersed after voting for the president, the Electoral College did not threaten the independence of the executive. With only minor adjustments—most notably, the House replaced the Senate as the body that would select the president if a majority of electors failed to agree on a candidate—the convention endorsed the proposal.

The point of all this is that the Electoral College did not emerge because of opposition to popular election of the president. In his 2019 article "The Electoral College's Racist Origins," Wilfred Codrington III questions whether a color-blind political system is possible under our Constitution. If it is, the Supreme Court's evisceration of the Voting Rights Act in 2013, he noted, did little to help matters. He further noted that while black people in America today are not experiencing 1950s levels of voter suppression, efforts to keep them and other citizens from participating in elections began within twenty-four hours of the Shelby County v. Holder ruling and have only increased since then.

In Shelby County's oral argument, Justice Antonin Scalia cautioned, "Whenever a society adopts racial entitlements, it is very difficult to get them out through the normal political processes." Ironically enough, there is some truth to an otherwise frighteningly numb claim. American elections have an acute history of racial entitlements; only they don't privilege black Americans.

For centuries, white votes have gotten undue weight as a result of innovations such as poll taxes and voter-ID laws and outright violence to discourage racial minorities from voting. The point was obvious to anyone paying attention: As William F. Buckley argued in his essay "Why the South Must Prevail," white Americans are "entitled to take such measures as are necessary to prevail, politically and culturally," anywhere they are outnumbered because they are part of "the advanced race." But America's institutions boosted white political power in less obvious ways, too, and the nation's oldest structural racial entitlement program is one of its most consequential: the Electoral College.

Mistake Number 2: Another common belief is that the convention rejected popular election of the president because the delegates feared majority tyranny. People make this claim as though to say that because the framers were skittish of a national popular election, so should we be today. But, once again, this interpretation of history is wrong. The convention did twice reject popular election of the president. But the delegates who rejected it did not object to popular elections per se; they had no problem with popular election of the House of Representatives or state legislatures. Rather, they were skeptical of a national popular election, primarily for reasons that are no longer relevant today.

First, they feared that people would lack the information to make an informed choice as to who might be an appropriate candidate for the presidency or who might be the best choice among candidates. Thus, George Mason of Virginia claimed, "It would be as unnatural to refer the choice of a proper candidate for chief Magistrate to the people, as it would be to refer a trial of colors to a blind man." But his reason was that "the extent of the country renders it impossible that the people can have the requisite capacity to judge of the respective pretensions of the candidates." In such circumstances, he thought, voters would naturally gravitate toward candidates from their own state. Delegates who favored popular election replied that "the increasing intercourse among the people of the states would render important characters less and less unknown," and that "continental characters will multiply as we more or more coalesce," reducing state parochialism. Today, with mass communication and interminable campaigns, lack of information is no longer a problem.

Second, some southern delegates feared that popular election of the president would disadvantage their states. James Madison noted that, given less restrictive voting laws, "The right of suffrage was much more diffusive in the Northern than the Southern states," which would give them an advantage in a popular election. Beyond that, a popular vote would not count the disenfranchised enslaved population, reducing southern influence.

The Electoral College solved both those problems, awarding electoral votes based on a state's population, not its electorate, and importing the three-fifths compromise into presidential elections. The effects were immediate and dramatic: In 1800, John Adams would have defeated Thomas Jefferson had only free persons been counted in awarding electoral votes. Obviously, these concerns no longer apply, although popular election would encourage states to increase their influence by expanding their electorate, while the Electoral College offers no such incentive.

Third, some small-state delegates opposed popular election because they feared that larger states, with their greater voting power, would dominate. Yet these same delegates also objected to the Electoral College, insisting it too gave excessive power to the large states. Their concerns were addressed by stipulating that should no candidate receive a majority of the electoral vote, the selection would devolve on the House of Representatives, with each state casting a single vote.

What is striking about the convention's debate on popular election of the president is that its opponents did not claim it would encourage majority tyranny. Doubtless the delegates were aware of the danger of such a tyranny; Madison first presented his famous discussion of "majority faction" at the convention, but no delegate objected to popular election on that basis, and Madison himself supported popular election of the president.

According to Peter Beinart, November 21, 2016: "The Electoral College was Meant to Stop Men Like Trump from Being President." The founders, he explained, envisioned electors as people who could prevent an irresponsible demagogue from taking office. Americans talk about democracy like it's sacred. In public discourse, the more democratic American government is, the better.

The people are supposed to rule. But that's not the premise that underlies America's political system. Most of the men who founded the United States feared unfettered majority rule. James Madison wrote in "Federalist 10" that systems of government based upon "pure democracy [...] have ever been found incompatible with personal security or the rights of property." John Adams wrote in 1814 that, "Democracy never lasts long. It soon wastes, exhausts and murders itself."

The framers constructed a system that had democratic features. The people had a voice. They could, for instance, directly elect members of the House of Representatives. But the founders also self-consciously limited the people's voice.

The Bill of Rights is undemocratic. It limits the federal government's power in profound ways—ways the people often dislike. Yet the people can do almost nothing about it. The Supreme Court is undemocratic, too. Yes, the people elect the president (kind of), who appoints justices of the Supreme Court, subject to approval by the Senate, which these days is directly elected, too. But after that, the justices wield their extraordinary power for as long as they wish without any democratic accountability. The vast majority of Americans may desperately want their government to do something. The Supreme Court can say no. The people then lose unless they pass a constitutional amendment, which is extraordinarily difficult, or those Supreme Court justices die. That's the way the framers wanted it. And, oddly, it's the way most contemporary Americans want it, too. Americans say they revere democracy. Yet they also revere those rights (freedom of speech, freedom of religion, the right to bear arms) that the government's least democratic institutions protect. Americans rarely contemplate these contradictions. If they did, they might have been more open to preventing Donald Trump from becoming the president: the kind of democratic catastrophe that the Constitution, and the Electoral College in particular, were in part designed to prevent.

Donald Trump was not elected on November 8. Under the Constitution, the real election will occur on December 19. That's when the electors in each state cast their votes. The Constitution says nothing about the people as a whole electing the president. It says in Article II that "Each State shall appoint, in such Manner as the Legislature thereof may direct, a Number of Electors." Those electors then vote for president and vice-president. They can be selected "in such Manner as the Legislature thereof may direct." Which is to say, any way the state legislature wants. In fourteen states in the early 19th century, state legislatures chose their electors directly. The people did not vote at all.

This ambiguity about how to choose the electors was the result of a compromise. James Madison and some other framers favored some manner of popular vote for president. Others passionately opposed it. Some of the framers wanted Congress to choose the president. Many white southerners supported the Electoral College because it counted their non-voting slaves as three-fifths of a person, and thus gave the South more influence than it would have enjoyed in a national vote. The founders compromised by leaving it up to state legislatures. State legislatures could hand over the selection of electors to the people as a whole. In that case, the people would have a voice in choosing their president. But—and here's the crucial point—the people's voice would still not be absolute. No matter how they were selected, the electors would retain the independence to make their own choice.

It is "desirable," Alexander Hamilton wrote in "Federalist 68," "that the sense of the people should operate in the choice of" president. But it is "equally desirable, that the immediate election should be made by men most capable of analyzing the qualities adapted to the station." These "men" (the electors) would be "most likely to possess the information and discernment requisite to such complicated investigations." And because of their discernment, because they possessed wisdom that the people as a whole might not, "the office of President will never fall to the lot of any man who is not in an eminent degree endowed with the requisite qualifications."

As Michael Signer explains, the framers were particularly afraid of the people choosing a demagogue. The electors, Hamilton believed, would prevent someone with "talents for low intrigue, and the little arts of popularity" from becoming president. And they would combat "the desire in foreign powers to gain an improper ascendant in our councils." They would prevent America's adversaries from meddling in its elections. The founders created the Electoral College, in other words, in part to prevent the election of someone like Donald Trump.

To modern American ears, it sounds insanely undemocratic for electors to ignore the will of the people of their state. But were Hamilton alive, he might wonder why Americans find this undemocratic feature of the Electoral College so outrageous while taking its other undemocratic features virtually for granted. For instance, each state gets as many electors as it has members of the House of Representatives and Senate. (The District of Columbia now gets a few, too). That is itself undemocratic. It's undemocratic because while representatives are allocated between the states via population, senators are not. Each state gets two, whether it has thirty-eight million people (California) or half a million (Wyoming). Because states, not people, are represented equally in the Senate, the Senate is undemocratic. And because a state's number of electors is based partly on its number of senators, the Electoral College is thus partially undemocratic, too.

Moreover, every state except Nebraska and Maine allocates its electors based on the principle of winner take all. Win California by one vote and you get all its electors. For that reason, too, the Electoral College does not always reflect the popular vote. In two of the last five presidential elections, in fact, the candidate who received the most votes, Al Gore, in 2000 and Hillary Clinton in 2016, has lost the Electoral College. Americans are mildly but not profoundly disturbed by this. Most of the people protesting Donald Trump's election are not protesting because he lost the popular vote. When George W. Bush became president after losing the popular vote in 2000, there were protests, but no real question about the inevitability of his taking office. In this way, as in many others, Americans comfortably accept undemocratic elements of America's system of government even as they profess publicly that democracy is sacrosanct.

In truth, Americans are wedded less to democracy than to familiarity. They accept those undemocratic features of the Electoral College, and of American government in general, to which they're accustomed. They value things as they are. This makes sense. Americans are used to choosing presidents in a particular way. As the University of Michigan constitutional law professor Richard Primus pointed out to me, they're like a family that for as long as anyone can remember has been playing a board game by a certain set of rules. What happens if, in the middle of a game, one player consults the instructions, finds that the actual rules are different, and proposes suddenly abiding by them instead? The other players, especially those who would be disadvantaged by the change, will likely refuse.

Were the electors to meet on December 19 and decide that Donald Trump is unfit to be president, all hell would break loose. Trump's supporters, and even some who opposed him, would say the election had been stolen. Their worst fears about America's "rigged" system of government would be confirmed. The president whom the electors chose, even if it were Hillary Clinton, who beat Trump by over a million votes, would lack legitimacy in the eyes of much of the public. It's unclear whether such a president could effectively govern. Violence might break out. Moreover, once the precedent was set, future electors would become more likely to act independently again. The process of choosing them would grow fraught. America's entire system of presidential elections would grow unstable.

It's a terrifying prospect. The prospect of a Trump presidency, however, is terrifying too: terrifying in unprecedented ways. Which is why, for the first time in modern American history, there's a plausible case for urging the electors to vote their consciences. The case is not overwhelming. But it's not absurd. It all depends on how dangerous you think President Trump would be.

Could the danger posed by electing Trump exceed the enormous danger posed by stopping him? It could, for four reasons:

The first is climate change. Trump has repeatedly called it a "hoax." He's vowed to "cancel" America's obligations under the climate agreement signed last year in Paris, which might lead other nations to do the same, and to undo the restrictions on emissions from coal-fired power plants instituted by the Obama administration. According to a study by Lux Research, America's annual carbon emissions, which would have dropped under a Clinton presidency, will rise sharply under Trump. And if emissions don't drop, an article this spring in the journal *Nature* predicts that thirteen million Americans who live in coastal areas could find their communities uninhabitable over the next century. Half of Florida's population would be at risk.

The second reason to think that allowing a Trump presidency might be more dangerous than overturning it is the threat of nuclear war. At several points over the last seventy years, presidents have faced decisions that could have triggered nuclear catastrophe. Harry Truman considered dropping atomic bombs on North Korea in 1950. John F. Kennedy famously said during the Cuban missile crisis that the chances of war with the Soviet Union were "between 1 in 3 and even." According to Israeli historian Dmitry Adamsky, the Reagan administration's 1983 war game, Able Archer, which the Soviets misinterpreted as preparation for an American attack, "almost became a prelude to a preventative nuclear strike." As Jeffrey Goldberg has noted, North Korea (the most bellicose and erratic regime on earth) may have nuclear missiles that can reach the U.S. mainland by the end of Trump's second term, which increases the chances that he could face his own moment of nuclear reckoning. In August, MSNBC's Joe Scarborough reported that, during a private meeting with a "foreign policy expert," Trump had asked the expert "three times, in an hour briefing, 'Why can't we use nuclear weapons?'" In March, Trump asked Chris Matthews, "Somebody hits us within ISIS, you wouldn't fight back with a nuke?" Trump has also repeatedly declared his desire to be "unpredictable" when it comes to the use of nuclear weapons.

The president can launch nuclear weapons within minutes, on his own authority. In the words of former National Security Agency Director Michael Hayden, "The system is designed for speed and decisiveness. It's not designed to debate the decision." Trump is famous for his impulsivity (his self-destructive late night tweets almost cost him the presidential race), his policy ignorance (he twice during the campaign seemed unaware that the U.S. has nuclear weapons on air, land, and sea), and his dismissive attitude toward experts (in November he boasted that, "I know more about ISIS than the generals do.") This is why fifty former Republican national security officials warned in August that he "would be the most reckless president in American history."

Does all this mean that, under President Trump, nuclear war is likely? No. But it does mean that it's significantly more likely than it would have been under Hillary Clinton or any other plausible alternative.

The third reason it's not crazy for electors to consider defying the popular will in their states is the prospect of what Trump might do in the event of a terrorist attack. Last November, Trump said he'd require Muslims to register in a government database. In December, after jihadist terrorists killed fourteen people and seriously injured twenty-two in San Bernardino, California, he demanded a "total and complete shutdown of Muslims entering the United States until our country's representatives can figure out what is going on."

Trump has also barred numerous reporters from his rallies, vowed to make it easier to sue journalists for libel, and called for investigating *Washington Post* owner Jeff Bezos' tax returns in retaliation for his paper's critical coverage of Trump's campaign.

What might President Trump do if terrorists killed hundreds or even thousands on American soil? During times of war and cold war, even more sober presidents have massively violated individual freedoms. During World War I, Woodrow Wilson signed the Sedition Act, which made "uttering, printing, writing, or publishing any disloyal, profane, scurrilous, or abusive language about the United States government or military" a crime. FDR interned Japanese-Americans during World War II. John F. Kennedy allowed J. Edgar Hoover to bug Martin Luther King's phone. We don't know how Trump would respond in a moment of national hysteria, when restricting press freedom and persecuting unpopular minorities can become seductively easy. We do know that, based on his past statements, he'd be less restrained by the Bill of Rights than any other president in recent memory.

The final reason it's worth debating an Electoral College rejection of Trump is the potential that his presidency could spark a constitutional crisis. During the campaign, in a stunning break from American tradition, Trump repeatedly suggested that he might not accept the outcome. As one Trump ally told *Politico*, "If he loses, [he'll say] 'It's a rigged election' […] I can't really picture him giving a concession speech, whatever the final margin."

If defeated in his bid for a second term, would Trump leave the White House? Would he leave if Congress impeached him? Would he abide by a decision of the Supreme Court that thwarted his agenda? "I can easily see a situation in which he would take the Andrew Jackson line," declared the eminent libertarian-conservative legal scholar Richard Epstein in June. "[Chief Justice] John Marshall has made his decision; now let him enforce it." The problem with all these hypothetical scenarios is that they're just that: hypothetical. The dangers posed by a Trump presidency are speculative. The dangers posed by using the Electoral College to forestall a Trump presidency are more certain. Moreover, some of the very characteristics that make a Trump presidency so frightening also make his response to being defeated by the electors frightening. If Trump was prepared to contest defeat on November 8, it's hard to imagine him accepting it on December 19.

Luckily for Trump, the chances of the electors actually defeating him on that date are extremely slim. Two electors from states that supported Hillary Clinton are reportedly trying to convince their colleagues from states that supported Trump to vote for other Republicans, thus denying Trump a majority and sending the presidential election to the House of Representatives. But these days, electors are not the independent-minded figures Hamilton envisioned. They're party activists chosen for their loyalty. Many states even have laws requiring electors to abide by the popular vote, though David Pozen, a law professor at Columbia (and author of a smart recent blog post on Trump and the Electoral College) told me that such laws may well be unconstitutional.

If it's so unlikely that the electors would defeat Trump, why is the topic even worth discussing? Because, given Trump's likely ascension to the presidency, Americans must talk differently about democracy itself. Yes, the democratic features of America's political system are precious. But so are some of the undemocratic ones: the ones that prevent people's basic rights from being taken from them by a show of hands. Right now, the nature of American public discourse, which treats democracy as an unambiguous good, makes that difficult to say. Rarely do Americans publicly acknowledge the tradeoff between democracy and liberty, between popular will and minority rights, which so concerned the framers. If Trump threatens the rights of Muslims or journalists, if he pressures the Federal Reserve or defies the Supreme Court, he will likely do so in democracy's name. He may have public opinion on his side. If Americans can't defend their system's limitations on democracy, they'll have trouble resisting him.

Democracy is a crucial component of American government. But, as Fareed Zakaria has argued, more democracy isn't always better. For most of American history, political parties were not internally democratic. They aren't in most democracies around the world, either. Yet during the primaries, when GOP elites sought to block Trump's nomination, the media generally described their efforts as undemocratic, which made them almost impossible to publicly defend. I didn't defend them either. I was wrong. Before this election, I supported abolishing the Electoral College. Now I think America needs electors who, in times of national emergency, can prevent demagogues from taking power.

Go ahead and call me an elitist; Donald Trump has changed the way I view American government. Before this year, I would have considered Hamilton's demand for independent-minded electors who could prevent candidates with "talents for low intrigue, and the little arts of popularity" from winning the presidency to be antiquated and retrograde. Now I think the framers were prescient and I was naïve. Eighteen months ago, I could never have imagined President Donald Trump. Now I'm grateful that, two hundred and twenty-seven years ago, they did.

Mistake Number 3: Similarly, some defenders of the Electoral College have argued that the delegates who favored the Electoral College opposed popular election of the president. Given the current debate on presidential selection, this might seem obvious, but the deliberations at the convention were much more fluid. James Wilson of Pennsylvania first proposed popular election of the president, but when his motion failed, he immediately raised the possibility of a mediated popular election: electors chosen by the people who would select the executive. All the other leading advocates of popular election (Morris, Madison, and Alexander Hamilton) also supported the Electoral College, primarily as an alternative to congressional selection. In defending the Electoral College, Madison and Hamilton emphasized its popular character. Madison in "Federalist No. 39" noted that "the President is indirectly derived from the choice of the people," and Hamilton in "Federalist No. 68" concurred: "The sense of the people should operate in the choice of the person to whom so important a trust was to be confided," and reelection should depend on "the people themselves."

Mistake Number 4: Many people also believe that the Electoral College was designed to preserve federalism and states' rights. The Constitution was, in James Madison's words, "in strictness neither a national nor a federal Constitution, but a composition of both." It empowered state legislatures to determine how the presidential electors were to be chosen, and if the Electoral College failed to select a president, the House of Representatives would do so, with each state casting a single vote. However, the debates during the Constitutional Convention make clear that the Electoral College was not intended to protect the states or enhance the influence of state governments and state perspectives.

The convention delegates sought to safeguard the independence of the national executive from state governments. They overwhelmingly rejected proposals that the executive be selected by state legislatures or by state governors. They also rejected a proposal that the president be removable upon request by a majority of state legislatures and did not even consider the New Jersey Plan's provision that the president "be recalled by Congress when requested by the majority of executive of the states." This was hardly surprising. Most delegates were sharply critical of state legislatures and wanted to ensure that the president had the independence necessary to oppose their schemes. Madison summarized the prevailing sentiment: "The President is to act for the people, not the States.

Although the Electoral College allowed state legislatures to determine how electors would be chosen, it was expected that once selected, the electors would operate independently of their state governments. The constitutional ban on senators serving as electors and the choice of the House to resolve deadlocks in the Electoral College ensured that those selected by (and perhaps influenced by) state legislatures would not play a role in selecting the president. Beyond that, the delegates expected that the electors' deliberations would remain secret, that they would be free to choose the candidates they believed most qualified, and that their votes would be tabulated and transmitted to the president of the Senate without any indication as to who voted for which candidate, so that no political retribution could be exacted. The Constitution's requirement that electors vote for two candidates (at least one of whom was not from their state) served to reduce state parochialism and encourage a national perspective.

In sum, the Electoral College was not designed to promote federalism. Martin Diamond, one of the most thoughtful proponents of the Electoral College, accurately described the design as "an anti-states-rights device, a way of keeping the election from state politicians and giving it to the people." The core protections of federalism, today as in the past, are the vitality of state governments, the division of powers between nation and state, and representation in Congress along state lines. The replacement of the Electoral College by a nationwide popular vote would threaten none of these. Voting procedures would remain the same, the only difference being that votes would be tabulated nationwide rather than state by state.

Mistake Number 5: And finally, perhaps the most widely believed and, at the same time, most incorrect of the arguments for the Electoral College is that it has vindicated the hopes and expectations of its creators. To begin with, to some extent those expectations were unclear. For example, after the Electoral College was proposed, some delegates claimed that in most elections (George Mason predicted "nineteen times in twenty") no candidate would get a majority of the electoral votes, and so the House of Representatives would elect the president. This of course would compromise the independence of the executive, and both Madison and Hamilton unsuccessfully proposed that the House's role be eliminated, with the candidate winning a plurality of the electoral vote becoming president. Other delegates expected that a majority of the electors would coalesce around a single candidate. In "Federalist No. 39," Madison presumed that "the eventual election" would be made by the House, but this was mere speculation and quickly disproved.

Even when the delegates' hopes and expectations were clear, constitutional amendments have altered the operation of the Electoral College. The Twelfth Amendment, adopted after the contested election of 1800, requires electors to specify for whom they are voting for president and vice president. The Twentieth Amendment, by shifting the date congressional terms begin to January 3, ensures that the newly elected House of Representatives, rather than the previous House, would elect the president if no candidate received an electoral-vote majority. And the Twenty-Third Amendment extends the right to vote in presidential elections to U.S. citizens residing in the District of Columbia, awarding the District three electoral votes, though the Electoral College continues to deny American citizens living in Puerto Rico and other U.S. territories any role in choosing the president.

Even more important have been changes in political practice. In "Federalist No. 64," John Jay maintained that the Electoral College "will in general be composed of the most enlightened and respectable citizens," and in "Federalist No. 68," Alexander Hamilton described the electors as "most likely to possess the information and discernment" necessary to choose the chief executive. But by 1800 political parties had developed, and elector discretion was replaced by elector commitment to the parties' candidates. Today many states do not even bother to list the electors' names on the ballot. Interestingly, Hamilton and Madison as party leaders played a crucial role in this transformation.

The Constitution authorized state legislatures to determine how electors were to be selected, but by 1828 every state but South Carolina chose its electors by popular vote, and today all states do. Moreover, despite the initial expectation that electors would be chosen in districts, by 1836 party competition had promoted a winner-take-all allocation of electors in all the states. (Maine and Nebraska have since bucked that trend.) This in turn has affected presidential campaigns, as more and more candidates target their speeches, campaign appearances, and ads at "swing states" and largely ignore states they confidently expect to carry or to lose.

Meanwhile, the proliferation of primary elections, the nationalization of the choice of presidential candidates, the move toward candidate-based campaigns, and the reduced importance of state party organizations have fundamentally transformed presidential selection, without changing how votes are awarded under the Electoral College. In "Federalist No. 68," Alexander Hamilton contended that the Electoral College would frustrate "the desire in foreign powers to gain an improper ascendant in our councils." It would also "afford a moral certainty that the office of President would seldom fall to the lot of any man who is not in an eminent degree endowed with the requisite qualifications." In addition, it would keep from the office candidates with "talents for low intrigue, and the little arts of popularity." In evaluating the Electoral College today, one must judge whether Hamilton's hopes have been vindicated. It would be a real stretch to even suggest that Hamilton's hopes have been vindicated. The Electoral College is, by every measure, an abject failure. Who knew that the Electoral College is the nation's oldest structural racial entitlement program and one of its most consequential? Those in power would have you believe that entitlement programs are tools the Democrats use as giveaways to black and brown people. American elections have an acute history of racial entitlements; only they don't privilege black or brown Americans. It's a white thing, because they are 'the advanced race.' You can't make this stuff up.

Chapter Eight
Medicare for All Health Plan

According to the Kaiser Family Foundation, a narrow majority of Americans favors a national "Medicare for All" health plan, according to a new poll, but even more like a public option. The poll, released Thursday by the Kaiser Family Foundation, found that 56 percent of respondents said they want Medicare for All, while 68 percent said they favored a public option that competes alongside private insurance. There is some bipartisan support as well. While most Republicans oppose both plans, 42 percent said they support a public option. Among Democrats and independents, there were strong preferences for both types of health coverage plans. The poll found that 77 percent of Democratic respondents, and 66 percent of independents, said they support Medicare for All. In addition, an overwhelming 85 percent of Democrats and 73 percent of independents said they support a public option. Democratic candidates have been attacking each other for months over which type of health plan is best. While other polls have shown sharp divisions over Medicare for All in certain states, this latest Kaiser poll shows a growing acceptance of the progressive policy. However, a public option, like the plan championed by former Vice President Joe Biden, remains overall more popular than Medicare for All.

The poll also found that following six months of news coverage of the Democratic presidential debates and campaigns, the public was more aware of the potential impacts of Medicare for All than they were erstwhile. For example, more people said they understand that a public option would keep employer-sponsored insurance, while Medicare for All would not.

Separately, the poll found the public gives President Trump low numbers on health care issues. Only 30 percent of respondents said they approved of how Trump is handling prescription drug costs, while 35 percent said they approved of his handling of the Affordable Care Act, protecting people with pre-existing conditions, and Medicaid. (Kaiser polled 1,212 adults; the results have a 3 percentage point margin of error).

～

The Difference Between A 'Public Option' And 'Medicare For All'?

Democrats, the many running for president as well as energized members of Congress, are talking big about health care again. Among other things, that means brace yourself for some jargon. Here's your neighborhood health care nerd to help define some terms.

Various proposals are floating around, each of which would change the health care system in distinct ways. Some, like one from Senator Bernie Sanders, would do away with all private health insurance. Some would make small expansions in existing public programs. Some would try to cover all Americans through a mix of different insurance types. It can be mystifying when people call all of these ideas "Medicare for All," as some in the debate have been doing.

A glossary of terms could make the debate less confusing. Let's start with the basics.

What is Medicare?

Medicare is a fifty-four-year-old program that provides health insurance for Americans aged sixty-five and older, and for a few other groups of people with particular diseases or disabilities.

Traditional Medicare pays doctors and hospitals according to set prices determined by the government, and most medical providers in the United States accept it. It's also possible to enroll in private Medicare plans that can offer additional benefits, though with a more limited set of health providers.

Private plans handle Medicare drug coverage, and you can choose among options. You pay premiums each year, and you pay deductibles and co-payments when you use medical services.

Because the program's out-of-pocket spending has no limits, most Medicare beneficiaries also buy private supplemental insurance to limit those costs. That insurance doesn't cover medical services outside the Medicare system, but it helps pay the patient's share of the bill when a person goes to the doctor or hospital.

~~~

WHAT IS MEDICARE FOR ALL?

This increasingly popular term was coined to describe a system in which all Americans, not just older ones, get health insurance through the government's Medicare system. Mr. Sanders, who prominently featured such a plan in his 2016 presidential platform and just announced he has joined the 2020 race, uses this term a lot. His plan would both expand traditional Medicare to cover all Americans and change the structure of the program to cover more services and eliminate most deductibles and co-payments. So, the Medicare everyone would be getting would differ in crucial ways from the Medicare older people get now.

There would effectively be no private health insurance because the new system would cover everyone and everything; duplicative coverage would be banned. That's why Senator Kamala Harris of California, a co-sponsor of the Sanders bill and a presidential candidate, told CNN recently that she would endorse abolishing all private insurance; doing so is a key feature of the plan.

But there are many other possible flavors of Medicare for All. Though no prominent politicians are currently proposing it, an expansion of the current Medicare benefits—with its current co-payments, deductibles, and premiums—could also be thought of as "Medicare for All."

The idea of Medicare for All is suggestive of the health care system in Canada. There, doctors and hospitals remain private, but everyone gets insurance from the government. No one there is asked to pay any money when seeing a doctor. The Canadian health care system is even called Medicare.

~~~

SINGLE-PAYER HEALTH CARE

This one is pretty simple if you understand Medicare for All. Single-payer is a more general term used to describe a government system, typically backed by taxes, in which everyone gets health care from one insurer, run by the government. Think of Medicare for All as a brand-name single-payer plan. Some advocates also like the term "national health insurance." These terms all describe a system in which the government pays for everyone's health care services.

~~~

SOCIALIZED MEDICINE

Critics of single-payer are particularly fond of this term, which describes a system in which the government runs not just the financing of health care (by running an insurance company like Medicare) but also manages hospitals and employs medical providers directly. Britain's National Health Service is an example of a socialized system. Doctors there work for the government.

The United States has its own socialized system, for military veterans. Veterans get their insurance through the Department of Veterans Affairs, which owns hospitals; employs doctors, nurses, and other medical professionals; and negotiates directly with pharmaceutical companies for drugs. In general, a veteran couldn't get coverage for routine care from a doctor who didn't work directly for the V.A., but recent policy changes have started to privatize more health care for veterans.

~~~

WHAT'S A PUBLIC OPTION

When lawmakers were writing the Affordable Care Act, there was an extensive debate about whether it should include a public option. The idea didn't prevail in the end, but many Democrats now want to bring it back. You can think of a public option as something of a compromise between a single-payer system and our current system, in which only certain Americans now qualify for government-run programs. More people, maybe many more, could get government insurance. But only if they wanted it. Public-option plans would allow middle-income, working-age adults to choose a public insurance plan (like Medicare or Medicaid) instead of a private insurance plan. There are various ways this could work. Some proposals would allow individuals to pay a premium to buy a Medicare or Medicaid plan that would be the same as the insurance now available to older people, the disabled, or the poor. Others would set up a new public plan, run by the government, that Americans could buy. Under most proposals, people who get federal help buying Obamacare coverage could use their government subsidies to help them buy either a private or public option. Most of the current proposals would limit access to the public option to certain groups of Americans. A bill from Senator Debbie Stabenow of Michigan and colleagues would allow only those older than fifty to buy a Medicare plan, for example. Some plans would allow only people who buy their own health insurance to choose Medicare or Medicaid as an option alongside those offered in the Obamacare exchanges.

Others would also let employers choose Medicare, instead of a private health insurance company, when offering benefits to their workers. A plan from a liberal think tank, the Center for American Progress, would make the public Medicare option available to anyone who wanted to sign up.

An advantage of a public option, at least politically, is it would preserve more choice for individuals, who could stick with a private plan if they prefer. That would make it less disruptive than a single-payer plan. A downside is that keeping lots of different insurance options could undermine one of the goals of a single-payer system: a simpler approach that would involve less money tied up in paperwork and insurance company profits.

~~~

UNIVERSAL COVERAGE

All of the earlier entries describe ways of organizing the health insurance system. Universal coverage is a broader goal. When people push for universal coverage, they mean that everyone should have access to the health care system. You'll sometimes hear politicians say that health care should be a "right." That statement is an endorsement of universal coverage.

Most other developed countries embrace this idea: that health care should not be only for those who can afford it. But those countries have not all embraced single-payer approaches.

There are ways to achieve universal coverage that don't look like a single-payer system at all. Most European countries, for example, have systems with competing private health insurance plans, along with tight regulation and government subsidies that make the premiums affordable for everyone. This sort of European-style coverage is not prominent in our current policy debate.

Chapter Nine
Voting Bloc

As chronicled by Rachel Slade, author of *Into the Ranging Sea*, on September 13, 2018 in her article "The Most Powerful New Voting Bloc in America Doesn't Vote":

> "A voting bloc is a group of voters that are strongly motivated by a specific common concern or group of concerns to the point that such specific concerns tend to dominate their voting patterns, causing them to vote together in elections. Hispanics are often classified as a unitary voting bloc, but there are differences in political preferences within this community. For example, in the 2010 midterm elections—in spite of general Republican victories—sixty percent of Hispanics voted Democratic, while only thirty-eight percent voted Republican." (Beliefnet 2016).

〰

MASTER STATUS

Master status is a social status that is the primary socially-identifying characteristic of an individual, such as being the President. Thus, conflict theory is particularly interested in the various aspects of master status in social position: the primary identifying characteristic of an individual seen in terms of race or ethnicity, sex or gender, age, religion, ability or disability, and socioeconomic status. When we are analyzing any element of society from this perspective, we need to look at the structures of wealth, power and status, and the ways in which those structures maintain social, economic, political, and coercive power of one group at the expense of others.

According to conflict theorists, the family works toward the continuance of social inequality within a society by maintaining and reinforcing the status quo. Because inheritance, education, and social capital are transmitted through the family structure, wealthy families are able to keep their privileged social position for their members, while individuals from poor families are denied similar status. By derivation, it is absolutely essential that we know our voting bloc and vote accordingly. For example, if you are of the master status you're likely to understand that your party affiliation is the Republican party (policies geared to protect the very rich) because they legislate to maintain wealth and power for the very rich and for large, powerful corporations. Juxtaposed, impoverished, poor, or ostensibly middle-class voting bloc are less likely to understand or recognize which party supports their needs. This is largely due to how dexterously those of the master status control the narrative. More simply stated, the rich and powerful are good at deception. Though deceit (lying) they convince those of a lesser socioeconomic status that they support them. Let me be even more clear; the Republican party does not draft legislation in support of any group not termed 'master status.' When Republicans are forced to sign legislation that benefits the less privileged, they do it kicking and screaming and holding their nose the whole way. Your voting bloc is undeniably supported primarily by the Democratic party. Yet, in 2008, 48 percent of Asian Americans turned out to vote, but approximately 35 percent of them voted Republican. Being married to an Asian woman, I have firsthand knowledge, anecdotally, that Asian voting blocs are unitary, but are influenced more by the dominated narrative than by anything else. For example, in the 2016 Presidential election, most of my wife's family voted for Trump because their friends were voting for Trump, and their friends were voting for Trump because their boss at work was voting for Trump. If you live in Texas, your boss always votes Republican. Furthermore, every public place in Texas is tuned in to *Fox News* and nothing else. Therefore, the prevailing messaging in Texas is pro-Republican and misinformation at best.

~~~

YOUNG VOTERS

May I suggest that you get less of your news from social media followings and do more to engage through mainstream media sources? Read political columns of America's top political reporters for the *Washington Post*, *New York Times*, *Boston Globe*, and other national political papers. Local news outlets seem to be more partisan and area centric.

~~~

BASIC CIVICS

In 2014, 26 percent of eighth-graders scored "below basic" on the civics part of the National Assessment of Educational Progress, commonly called the Nation's Report Card. There is mounting evidence that it's the fault of our declining educational system. A 2016 survey by the Annenberg Public Policy Center found that only 26 percent of Americans can name all three branches of government, which was a significant decline from previous years.

Civic knowledge and public engagement are at an all-time low. Not surprisingly, public trust in government is at only 18 percent and voter participation has reached its lowest point since 1996. Without an understanding of the structure of government, rights and responsibilities, and methods of public engagement, civic literacy and voter apathy will continue to plague American democracy. Educators and schools have a unique opportunity and responsibility to ensure that young people become engaged and knowledgeable citizens. While the 2016 election brought a renewed interest in engagement among youth, only 23 percent of eighth-graders performed at or above the proficient level on the National Assessment of Educational Progress (NAEP) civics exam, and achievement levels have virtually stagnated since 1998.

The policy solution that has garnered the most momentum to improve civics in recent years is a standard that requires high school students to pass the U.S. citizenship exam before graduation. However, I'm in the camp of the critics of a mandatory civics exam who argue that the citizenship test does nothing to measure comprehension of the material. Furthermore, if you examine the content of the U.S. citizenship exam, you too will question its efficacy in improving civics standards in schools. All states must immediately adopt civics as a requirement for high school graduation, provide teachers with detailed civics curricula, offer community service as a graduation requirement, and increase the availability of Advance Placement (AP) U.S. government classes.

When civics education is taught effectively, it can equip students with the knowledge, skills, and disposition necessary to become informed and engaged citizens. That rightly suggests that the poor performance of our young people in the areas of civic matters is not as a result of any fault of their own. Educators must also remember that civics is not synonymous with history. While increasing history courses and service requirements are potential steps to augment students' background knowledge and skill sets, civics is a narrow and instrumental instruction that provides students with the agency to apply these skills. This analysis finds a wide variation in state requirements and levels of youth engagement. While this research highlights that no state currently provides sufficient and comprehensive civic education, there is reason to be optimistic that high-quality civics education can impact civic behavior.

The future in civics education is extremely bright. While models for civic education vary widely, innovative programs designed by states, nonprofits, and schools have chosen new ways to promote civics education and increase youth community engagement.

~~~

PUBLIC CHARTER SCHOOLS ENCOURAGE EXPERIMENTAL LEARNING

YES (Youth Engaged in Service) Prep Public Schools is a public charter network in Houston that implements civics and service learning into its curriculum. Students in YES Prep's schools complete service projects that are high-impact and grow students' leadership skills, including summer enrichment programs with community service; mentorships between older and younger students; student-run service trips; and fifty hours of required community service. The high schools also require an ethics course in the senior year that neatly ties into students' service projects. By teaching civics in tandem with experiential learning, YES Prep teachers, more often than traditional public or private school teachers, were "very confident" that their students learned "to be tolerant of people and groups who are different from themselves," "to understand concepts such as federalism, separation of powers, and checks and balances," and "to develop habits of community service such as volunteering and raising money for causes," according to the 2010 American Enterprise Institute Program on American Citizenship survey. As a charter network serving low-income students, its service-centered mission serves both the students and their communities.

The Cesar Chavez Public Charter Schools for Public Policy serve about 1,200 students through three campuses in Washington, D.C. Their proximity to the nation's capital provides a unique opportunity to engage students in a public policy-centered curriculum. Their public policy program encourages students "to see themselves as change agents for their communities…" While all high school students must take an American government class, they also have multiple opportunities to turn their civic knowledge into agency. Each year, students must complete an advocacy project where they apply what they learn in class to current events, as they address policy issues facing the Council of the District of Columbia, U.S. Congress, and the federal courts. In ninth and tenth grades, Cesar Chavez students also complete a long-term community action project, where they use their personal interests to conduct research and address a public policy issue. Perhaps, most importantly, students complete a two-and-a-half-week fellowship seminar in eleventh grade that provides them with career, networking, and civic skills. With multiple opportunities for civic action, in addition to civic learning, students learn how to contribute to their communities, brainstorm solutions to local and global challenges, and engage with policymakers. A 2011 study of the Capitol Hill campus showed that the action-oriented curriculum was effectively preparing students to use their political skills to demand change. Schools that specialize in student engagement not only instill a strong emphasis on civic education, but they also use tangible experience to prepare students to be the next generation of leaders.

~~~

CONCLUSION

There are many policy levers for advancing civic education in schools, including civics or U.S. government courses; civics curricula closely aligned to state standards; community service requirements; instruction of AP U.S. government; and civics exams. While many states have implemented civics exams or civics courses as graduation requirements, these requirements often are not accompanied by resources to ensure that they are effectively implemented. Few states provide service-learning opportunities or engage students in relevant project-based learning. In addition, few students are sufficiently prepared to pass the AP U.S. government exam.

Moreover, low rates of millennial voter participation and volunteerism indicate that schools have the opportunity to better prepare students to fulfill the responsibilities and privileges of citizenship. While this brief calls for increasing opportunities for U.S. government, civics, or service-learning education, these requirements are only as good as how they are taught. Service learning must go beyond an act of service to teach students to systemically address issues in their communities; civics exams must address critical thinking in addition to comprehension of materials; and civics and government courses should prepare every student with the tools to become engaged and effective citizens.

Innovative efforts, such as Generation Citizen's action civics programming and Judicially Speaking's guest lectures from civics experts, have allowed for small changes to make a big impact on how teachers educate the next generation of leaders. While some highlighted examples have successfully reformed civics, more states, districts, and schools should invest in comprehensive and action-oriented civics curricula to build students' capacity to become engaged and knowledgeable citizens.

Chapter Ten
Capitalism

Merriam-Webster's Dictionary defines capitalism as "an economic system in which a country's trade, industry, and profits are controlled by private companies, instead of by the state, or the people whose time and labor powers those companies."

Young voters want a societal shift toward socialism. Hence, they endorse Bernie Sanders' Democratic Socialist movement. They envision Democratic socialism as a tool that enables ordinary people to rise from poverty. But, more importantly, this is a movement in which the rich plutocrats no longer own everything. To that very point, Karl Marx has always been a political visionary of mine. Marx presciently warned that one day the proletariat would rise up against the plutocracy and demand a fairer share. Bernie Sanders' supporters are evidentiary that change is afoot and that Democratic Socialism has become increasingly popular among young people in a short period of time.

The juxtaposition is that capitalism has become markedly less popular among the younger generations. Our younger generations are increasingly more informed as a result of access. Increasingly, they see capitalism for what it truly is in America: 'crony capitalism.' They understand that those who tout capitalism and a free market economy are only for laissez-faire capitalism (abstention by governments from interfering in the workings of the free market) when it comes to regulations. Young people see it for what it is in actual practice: crony capitalism, an economic system in which businesses thrive, not as a result of risk, but rather a return of money amassed through a nexus between the business class and the political class (the state, or government). By derivation, they are for laissez-faire capitalism when it benefits them, and they are for private business and government partnerships when that benefits them. If it sounds like hypocrisy, and it looks like hypocrisy, it is hypocrisy plain and simple.

If you'll indulge my breviloquent opining or brief opinion, I would posit that capitalism as we know it will be short-lived in this generation and that Democratic socialism will be the death of it. Henceforth, a newly competitive work environment, supported by the state, will arise, and under Democratic socialism the minimum wage will finally be a living wage; and every American will have affordable health insurance; and college will be within reach of every American without the weight of indebtedness for life; and, dare I say, the Republican party will implode. Hence, the death of crony capitalism will be the death of the Republican party.

What a wonderful development that will be when crony capitalists and their unfair financial tool are brought down. A capitalist nation is dominated by the free market, which is an economic system in which both prices and production are dictated by corporations and private companies in competition with one another. Capitalism also places a heavy focus on private property, economic growth, freedom of choice, and limited government intervention. Generally, those to the right of the political spectrum tend to be pro-capitalist; those on the left veer toward anti-capitalism.

The kind of impact that capitalism has on your life depends on whether you're a worker or a boss. For someone who owns a company and employs other workers, capitalism may make sense: The more profits your company brings in, the more resources you have to share with your workers, which theoretically improves everyone's standard of living. It's all based on the principle of supply and demand, and in capitalism, consumption is king. The problem is that many capitalist bosses aren't great at sharing the wealth, which is why one of the major critiques of capitalism is that it is a huge driver of inequality, both social and economic.

Capitalism takes the position that "greed is good," which its supporters say is a positive thing because greed drives profits and profits drive innovation and product development, which means there are more choices available for those who can afford them.

Its opponents say that capitalism is, by nature, exploitative and leads to a brutally divided society that tramples the working classes in favor of fattening the rich's wallets. For an example in recent history, the Occupy Wall Street movement began as an anti-capitalist protest against "the 1%" (the richest of the rich of the capitalist class) and asked why they are allowed to grow fat and happy while twenty percent of all American children live in poverty.

They both are involved in determining the price and production of goods and services. On one hand, capitalism is focused on the creation of wealth and ownership of capital and factors of production, whereas a free market system is focused on the exchange of wealth, or goods and services.

Chapter Eleven
Free Market Economy

The United States is ostensibly the world's premier free market economy. Its economic output is greater than any other country that has a free market. China has the world's largest economy, but it relies on a 'command economy.' Proponents opine that free markets may not be perfect, but they are probably the best way to organize an economy.

In the U.S., the free market is purported to depends on capitalism to thrive. The law of supply and demand, to some degree, sets prices and distributes goods and services.

Proponents say that this fits right in with the American Dream. It states that each person has the right to pursue their own idea of happiness. That pursuit drives the entrepreneurial spirit that capitalism needs. The Founding Fathers said in the Declaration of Independence that each American should have an equal opportunity to pursue their personal vision. They structured the Constitution, the highest law in the land, to protect that right.

The Constitution also instructs the federal government to "promote the general welfare." The U.S. Constitution allows the government to use central planning in areas of vital importance to the nation's growth. That includes defense, telecommunications, and transportation. In 1935, the Social Security Act extended the definition of the general welfare. It included unemployment compensation, retirement income, and aid for mothers with dependent children. It was part of FDR's New Deal to get America out of the Great Depression.

Since then, Congress has extended the general welfare clause to many other areas. But the priorities remain: defense and the well-being of seniors, women, and children. If you look at the federal budget, it reflects these priorities. The most significant budget item is Social Security benefits at $1.1 trillion. The second largest is military spending. It's $934 billion in Fiscal Year 2021. That's if you add Overseas Contingency Operations to the Defense Department base budget. Also included are defense support departments such as Homeland Security and Veterans Administration. The nation's third-largest priority is health care. Medicare costs $679 billion, and Medicaid costs $418 billion.

As a result, many worry that America is becoming a socialist welfare state. Others warn that the country is a slave of the military-industrial complex. I would posit that neither of those asserted developments are the real culprits, but rather ostensible reasons designed to propagate fear.

Let's get real: Republicans realize that the United States is actually a mixed economy, including both free market and command economies. Whereby, America is by every measure a mixed economy and is better for it.

A free market economy can't coordinate a national defense plan. It also leaves vulnerable members of society without a safety net. Erstwhile, the Founding Fathers included assurance to protect each child's opportunity to pursue happiness. Furthermore, a mixed economy combines the best aspects of a free market economy with those of a command economy.

A command economy is where the government uses a central plan to manage prices and distribution. Countries that follow communism use the command economy, and interestingly, the U.S. does as well. So do monarchies, fascists, and other totalitarian regimes. When people think of a command economy, they call to mind Russia, China, Cuba, North Korea, or Iran. But even these countries have adopted the characteristics of a free market economy. They must compete against market pricing throughout the world. Only a free market gives them the flexibility to succeed in a globalized economy. They are becoming mixed economies as well.

Proponents of the purported free market would have us believe that the United States is losing its free market status because Congress is spending above its means. Federal revenue doesn't cover spending. Each year the deficit adds to the debt. The national debt is more than each the country's annual economic output. The debt-to-GDP ratio is more than 100 percent. That's beyond the World Bank's tipping point of 77 percent.

The concern is not "Is America no longer a free market economy?" It is that Congress continues to spend beyond its means on everything. It must find a way to restore the balance envisioned by our Founding Fathers, but not always on the backs of the poorest Americans. One way to do that is to shift spending priorities to more effectively create living-wage jobs. Defense spending only creates 8,555 jobs for every one billion dollars spent. It's not a good unemployment solution since so much is spent on technology instead. Half of those funds could go toward public works construction (infrastructure), which creates 19,795 jobs for every one billion dollars. Putting people back to work, at a living-wage rate, will create the demand and tax dollars needed to let free market grow faster. At the same time, spending should be capped at current levels. Over time, that will restore the debt-to-GDP ratio to a sustainable level.

The ideal and the principle of the free market economy, of capitalism rightly understood, were never fulfilled. What is called "capitalism" today is a distorted, twisted, and deformed system of increasingly limited market relationships, as well as market processes hampered and repressed by state controls and regulations. And overlying the entire system of interventionist "crony" capitalism are the ideologies of eighteenth-century mercantilism, nineteenth-century socialism and nationalism, and twentieth-century paternalistic welfare statism.

In this warped development and evolution of "historical capitalism," as Wilhelm Röpke called it, the institutions for a truly free market economy have either been undermined or prevented from emerging. At the same time, the principles and actual meaning of a free market economy have become increasingly misunderstood and lost. But it is the principles and the meaning of a free market economy that must be rediscovered if liberty is to be saved and the burden of "historical capitalism" is to be overcome.

Henceforward, the construct of rightwing rhetoric is meant to propagate a notional ideal. But a notional ideal is not the same as the actual ideal. They would have you believe that it is free market capitalism that helps make each man and woman a "captain" of their own fate, with the freedom about what work and employment to pursue, and the liberty to spend the income they earn in their own personal desiring way to live the life they value and want, and that gives meaning and purpose to their own life.

They would also like you to believe that no person need put up with humiliation, abuse or disrespect from a bureaucrat or political official who has control over their fate through the power of government planning, regulation, and redistribution. But, remember that they only oppose regulations when they are enforced in a manner that prevents them from doing whatever they want. They love regulating what the rest of us can and cannot do. Free market capitalism offers people opportunities and choices as consumers, workers, and producers, with the liberty to change course whenever the benefits from doing so seem to outweigh the costs in the eyes of the individual.

Similarly, they want us to believe that free market, or laissez-faire, capitalism makes this all possible because it rests on a deeper political philosophical foundation based on the idea and ideal of the right of the individual to his own life, to be lived as he desires and chooses, as long as he respects the equal right of others to do the same. The rub here is that they don't respect our equal rights. Furthermore, they wrongly suggest that free market capitalism insists that there is no higher "national interest" above the individual interests of the separate citizens of a free society. In a system of free market capitalism, government should no more control money and the banking system than a limited government should control the production and sale of shoes, soap, or salami. This is yet another instance of "too much big government" unless it is partnering with big business.

Additionally, they have the audacity to posit that free market capitalism calls for each individual's peacefully earned property and income to be respected and protected from plunder and theft, and that includes any created rationale and attempted justification to rob Peter to redistribute to Paul through the coercive power of government. Interestingly though, they have no objection to using the power of government to rob Paul to pay Peter whereby Paul is representative of the working class and Peter is the uber-wealthy.

They say that the good name of "capitalism" has to be recaptured and restored, just as the good name and concept of "liberalism," rightly understood, should be returned to the advocates of individual liberty and free enterprise. Does that also include the liberty to vote for those they constantly try to disenfranchise through gerrymandering? Does it include the liberty of black and brown people and poor white people in their pursuit of happiness and equality in this rigged system? Does it include the liberty of the least in our society to have access to good healthcare? Does it include the liberty of black and brown people to equal treatment by the law? Why it is that capitalism and liberalism are only used together when it to intended to sell an advantage for the most affluent in our society?

However, we do agree that this task requires friends of freedom to explain and make clear to others that what we live under today is not "capitalism" as it could be, should be, and properly really means. The reality of that "historical capitalism," about which Wilhelm Röpke spoke, is the "crony capitalism" that must be rejected and opposed so that free men may someday live under and benefit from the truly free market capitalism economy and command economy that comprises the mixed economy that is the only economic system consistent with a society of human liberty.

As previously explained, a command economy is where a central government makes economic decisions, e.g., in the U.S., the Federal Reserve sets a target federal funds rate eight times a year, based on prevailing economic conditions. The Federal Reserve raises or lowers interest rates through its regularly scheduled Federal Open Market Committee. That's the monetary policy arm of the Federal Reserve Banking System. The FOMC sets a target for the fed funds rate after reviewing current economic data. The fed funds rate is the interest rate banks charge each other for overnight loans. Those loans are called fed funds. Banks use these funds to meet the federal reserve requirement each night. If they don't have enough reserves, they will borrow the fed funds needed. Since the banks set the rate, the Fed is actually setting a target for this important interest rate. By law, the banks can set any rate they want. But this is rarely a problem for the Fed. Banks meet the Fed's target because the nation's central bank gives them several strong incentives to do so.

Another example whereby a central government makes economic decisions is in the U.S. government setting national priorities including mobilizing for war or generating robust economic growth. The U.S. economy clearly doesn't rely solely on the laws of supply and demand that operate in a market economy. In recent years, many centrally planned economies around the world began adding aspects of the market economy. The resultant mixed economy better achieves their goals; such is the case in these United States of America.

The federal government also owns control of businesses in the event of an emergency. The Defense Production Act (DPA) is the primary source of

Presidential authorities to expedite and expand the supply of resources from the U.S. industrial base to support military, energy, space, and homeland security programs. These are in industries deemed essential to the goals of the economy. That includes finance, utilities, and automotive. There is no domestic competition in these sectors. The government creates laws, regulations, and directives to enforce the central plan. Businesses follow the plan's production and hiring targets. They can't respond on their own to free market forces.

Chapter Twelve
Protectionism

Protectionism is the practice of following protectionist trade policies. A protectionist trade policy allows the government of a country to promote domestic producers, thereby boosting the domestic production of goods and services by imposing tariffs or otherwise limiting foreign goods and services in the marketplace.

Protectionist policies also allow the government to protect developing domestic industries from established foreign competitors via taxes or duties imposed on imports known as tariffs. Tariffs increase the price of imported goods in the domestic market, which, consequently, reduces the demand for them.

Quotas, restrictions on the volume of imports for a particular good or service over a period of time, are another form of protectionist policies. Quotas are known as a "non-tariff trade barrier." A constraint on the supply causes an increase in the prices of imported goods, reducing the demand in the domestic market.

Subsidies and standardization are other protectionist policies: Subsidies are negative taxes or tax credits that are given to domestic producers by the government. They create a discrepancy between the price faced by consumers and the price faced by producers. Standardization is where the government of a country requires all foreign products to adhere to certain guidelines. For instance, the government may demand that all imports meet a certain specific requirement. Standardization measures tend to reduce foreign products in the market.

An economy usually adopts protectionist policies to encourage domestic investment in a specific industry. For instance, tariffs on the foreign import of automobiles would encourage domestic producers to invest more resources in automobile production. In addition, nascent domestic automobile producers would not be at risk from established foreign automobile producers. Although domestic producers are better off, domestic consumers are worse off as a result of protectionist policies, as they may have to pay higher prices for some inferior goods or services. Protectionist policies therefore tend to be very popular with businesses and very unpopular with consumers.

Protectionism is when a country tries to shield its own industries from international competition. Historically, protectionism has been associated with countries trying to develop. The most common argument for protectionism is that before a country can compete internationally it needs time to develop its own industries. This is sometimes called the "infant industry argument." When a country closes off its borders to trade, it gets time to learn how to produce things for itself that it otherwise would have imported from abroad: a strategy called "import-substitution." If all goes according to plan, eventually the protected industry will get really good at what it does and will be able to stand up to foreign competition without government help.

The United States was one of the first countries to use protectionism to develop. Under the leadership of Alexander Hamilton, the young country imposed high tariffs on imported goods like machinery and textiles, and directly subsidized many emerging industries. As late as 1850, tariffs accounted for almost 95 percent of the country's total tax collection. After the second World War, the U.S. opened up and started promoting free trade around the world. Tariffs are now only about 1 percent of the U.S. government's revenue.

Economists fight about whether protectionism is a smart way to develop. Some point to cases like South Korea, Japan, or the United States and argue that limiting trade early on was a key part of their development. Others point to less successful attempts at import substitution in Latin America and Africa. Protectionism can also be used by developed economies to try to shield businesses and workers from foreign competition. That's what a lot of the free trade debate is about. I would posit that free trade should restrict American companies and not allow them to move their operations overseas for cheap labor. Whereby, any company that moves is taxed at a 25 percent higher rate than other American companies, creating a sort of "reverse protectionism" if you will. This amounts to free trade without greedy American companies taking advantage of laws currently design to allow them to cheat the free trade economy. We must insist on such simple legislation that our elected representatives are obviously reluctant to enact.

～

SUMMARY

Our Constitution was masterfully constructed and is crystal clear as to how we can keep our Republic. More importantly, we all must do our part, through our political participation (at every level) in the process that so many have suffered gravely in order that we may be able to participate. Clearly, the prescience of our Founding Fathers is undeniable. They provided us a framework whereby we, through full participation and assiduity, can forge adherence to the Constitutional statutory obligations of elected officials. By derivation, it is incumbent upon each of us to do everything within our power to hold our elected officials accountable for legislating and regulating in a bipartisan and timely manner.

Through this book, I have attempted to outline some of the things we must familiarize ourselves with and focus on so we can begin pushing our representatives to execute or reform in a way that allows the political process to work as it was intended by our founders. I began this book with the goal of urging more participation and providing reasons to do so. I also wanted to provide some pointers that I thought would be advantageous to your success. I hope that I have in some way been able to do just that.

Also, I chose the title of this book because it is representative of a real thing, "White Light; Yellow Light District Dynamics; The Socioeconomic Divide," that anyone can observe any night in whatever urban area they reside in these United States. However, "The Socioeconomic Divide" is exhibited in a number of ways other than the white lights and yellow lights. Our government, on every level, makes every financial decision based on the socioeconomic status of its constituents. Also, there are political and economic determinants of disease etiology (causation) and treatment. For example, according to the Centers for Disease Control and Prevention (CDC), 60 percent of premature deaths are associated with social, environmental, and behavioral circumstances.

Furthermore, I hope you are now better informed about the importance of basic civics education. Through civics we come to understand that we must make a hard push to get rid of the filibuster; stop redistricting and gerrymandering; effectuate simple majority voting and campaign finance reform; eliminate the Electoral College and encourage some form of health care that covers all of its citizens. I also hope that you now have an understanding of the American Experiment and its intent. I hope you have an understanding of the different voting blocs.

Finally, I sincerely hope that your understanding of capitalism, free markets, and protectionism motivates you to learn even more about why the system works better for one group at the expense of the other. And, I hope I have helped to motivate you in some small way to help take control of your own eventuality by participating in every political process on every level—starting immediately.

References

Allen, Mike; Birnbaum, Jeffrey H. (May 18, 2005). "A Likely Script for The 'Nuclear Option'". *The Washington Post*. ISSN 0190-8286. Retrieved January 23, 2017.

"Almanac of Theodore Roosevelt – Speeches of Theodore Roosevelt – Teddy Roosevelt". Theodore-roosevelt.com. Retrieved January 4, 2017.

AMERICAN HERITAGE: *The American Heritage Dictionary of the English Language*, New York, American Heritage Publishing Co., Inc., 1969.

"Americans Split on Whether NAFTA Is Good or Bad for U.S." Gallup.com. Retrieved April 22, 2018.

Annenberg Public Policy Center, "Americans' Knowledge of the Branches of Government Is Declining," September 13, 2016, available at https://www.annenbergpublicpolicycenter.org/americans-knowledge-of-the-branches-of-government-is-declining/. Pew Research Center.

"Archived copy". Archived from the original on February 25, 2017. Retrieved September 24, 2016.

Associated Press, "Lawmakers across US move to include young people in voting," WTOPFM, April 16, 2017, available at https://wtop.com/elections/2017/04/lawmakers-acrossus-move-to-include-young-people-in-voting/.

Author's calculations are based on data collected from the Education Commission of the States. Data are on file with author.

AYRES: Alfred Ayres, *The Verbalist: A Manual Devoted to Brief Discussions of the Right and the Wrong Use of Words and to Some Other Matters of*

Interest to Those Who Would Speak and Write with Propriety, New York, D. Appleton & Co., 1882.

Bach, Stanley (April 22, 2010). "Statement on Filibusters and Cloture: Hearing before the Senate Committee on Rules and Administration". *Examining the Filibuster: History of the Filibuster 1789–2008*. United States Senate Committee on Rules & Administration. pp. 5–7. Retrieved July 1, 2010.

Barbara M. Tucker, and Kenneth H. Tucker. *Industrializing Antebellum America: The Rise of Manufacturing Entrepreneurs in the Early Republic* (2008).

Bari Walsh, "Teaching Tolerance Today," Harvard Graduate School of Education, May 17, 2017, available at https://www.gse.harvard.edu/news/uk/17/05/teaching-tolerancetoday.

Barton, et al. *The Evolution of the Trade Regime: Politics, Law, and Economics of the GATT and the WTO* (2008).

Baumol, William J., Robert E. Litan, and Carl J. Schramm, 2007. *Good Capitalism, Bad Capitalism, and the Economics of Growth and Prosperity* (New Haven, Connecticut: Yale University Press).

Beale, Howard K. (1930). "The Tariff and Reconstruction". *American Historical Review*. 35 (2): 276–94. JSTOR 1837439.

Beliefnet. "The Twelve Tribes of American Politics." Beliefnet is a lifestyle website providing feature editorial content around the topics of inspiration, spirituality, health, wellness, love and family, news and entertainment., July 27, 2016. http://www.beliefnet.com/News/Politics/2004/10/The-Twelve-Tribes-Of-American-Politics.aspx.

Bernstein, William J. (2009). *A Splendid Exchange: How Trade Shaped the World*. Grove/Atlantic, Inc. p. 354. ISBN 978-1555848439.

Beth, Richard; Stanley Bach (December 24, 2014*). Filibusters and Cloture in the Senate* (PDF). Congressional Research Service. pp. 4, 9.

BIERCE: Ambrose Bierce. *Write It Right, A Little Blacklist of Literary Faults*, New York, Walter Neale, 1909.

Binder, Sarah (April 22, 2010). "The History of the Filibuster". Brookings. Retrieved June 14, 2012.

Binder, S. & Mann, T. (1995). "Slaying the dragon: The case for reforming the senate filibuster". *The Brookings Review*, 13(3), 42-46 Retrieved from http://www.jstor.org/discover/ 10.2307/20080580?uid=3739584 &uid=2&uid=4&uid=3739256&sid=21101256039901 Gold, M. (2008). Senate Procedure and Practice. Rowman & Littlefield.

Bolton, Alexander (January 24, 2013). "Liberals irate as Senate passes watered-down filibuster reform". *The Hill*. Retrieved January 31, 2013. Hearing on The History of the Filibuster: Hearing before the U.S. Senate Committee on Rules and Administration (testimony of Sarah Binders) retrieved from http://www.brookings.edu/research/testimony/2010/04/22-filibuster-binder

Bomboy, Scott. "On this day, Wilson's own rule helps defeat the Versailles Treaty - National Constitution Center". National Constitution Center – constitutioncenter.org. Retrieved May 15, 2019.

Books that are cited more than once in these pages are designated by a short label. A list of them follows:

Brauchli, Christopher (January 8–10, 2010). *A Helpless and Contemptible Body—How the Filibuster Emasculated the Senate*. CounterPunch.

Broz, J.L. (1999). "Origins of the Federal Reserve System: International Incentives and the Domestic Free-rider Problem". International Organization. 5353 (1): 39–46. doi: 10.1162/002081899550805.

BRYANT: Margaret M. Bryant. *Current American Usage*, New York, Funk & Wagnalls Co., Inc., 1962.

BRYANT: Margaret M. Bryant. *Modern English and Its Heritage, second edition*, New York, The Macmillan Company, 1962.

By Angela Pittenger, "Arizona civics test may keep 14 Tucson-area teens from graduating," Arizona Daily Star, May 21, 2017, available at http://tucson.com/news/local/education/arizona-civics-test-may-keep-tucson-area-teens-from-graduating/article_f511c65fef52-5804-9261-6fdadbc6fd42.html.

Cesar Chavez Schools, "Chavez Schools' Unique Programs," available at http:// www.chavezschools.org/programs/ (last accessed February 2018).

Cesar Chavez Schools, "History," available at http://www.chavezschools .org/history/ (last accessed February 2018).

"Changing the Rule". Filibuster. Washington, DC: CQ-Roll Call Group. 2010. Archived from the original on June 7, 2010. Retrieved June 24, 2010.

Chronicled and Hosted by Michael Barbaro, produced by Rachel Quester, Andy Mills, Clare Toeniskoetter and Jessica Cheung, and edited by Paige Cowett.

"Civil Rights Filibuster Ended". Art & History Historical Minutes. United States Senate. Retrieved March 1, 2010.

"Classic Speeches 1830 - 1993" (PDF). Senate.gov. Retrieved February 21, 2019.

COBBETT: *The English Grammar of William Cobbett Carefully Revised and Annotated by Alfred Ayres*, New York, D. Appleton and Company, 1891.

"Collected Works of Abraham Lincoln. Volume 1". Quod.lib.umich.edu. Retrieved January 4, 2017.

College Board, "AP Exam Volume Changes (2006–2016)," available at https://securemedia. collegeboard.org/digitalServices/pdf/research /2016/2016-Exam-Volume-Change.pdf (last accessed February 2017).

College Board, "Student Score Distributions, AP Exams – May 2016," available at https://secure-media.collegeboard.org/digitalServices/ pdf/research/2016/Student-Score-Distributions-2016.pdf (last accessed February 2018).

Colorado Department of Education, "Developing Colorado's High School Graduation Requirements," available at http://www.cde.state. co.us/postsecondary/graduationguidelines (last accessed February 2018).

Corporation for National and Community Service, "National Trends and Highlights Overview," available at https://www.nationalservice. gov/vcla/national (last accessed February 2018.

COWLES: Cowles Volume Library, New York, Cowles Book Company, Inc., 1969.

CURME: George O. Curme. *Syntax*. Boston, D. C. Heath and Company, 1931.

David W. Detzer, "Businessmen, Reformers, and Tariff Revision: The Payne-Aldrich Tariff of 1909", Historian, (1973) 35#2 pp. 196–204, online.

Department of State. The Office of Electronic Information, Bureau of Public Affairs (February 6, 2017). (PDF). Fpc.state.gov. Retrieved February 21, 2019.

Dewey. *Financial History of the United States* (5th ed. 1915) ch. 1–6.

Douglas A. Fisher. *Steel Serves the Nation, U.S. Steel, 1951*, pp. 15, 48.

Douglas A. Irwin, "The Aftermath of Hamilton's 'Report on Manufactures'", *Journal of Economic History*, Sept 2004, Vol. 64, Issue 3, pp. 800–21.

Edward S. Kaplan. *American Trade Policy: 1923–1995* (1996).

Eric Bradner. "Trump, Sanders and the protectionist revolution". Cnn.com. Retrieved March 24, 2017.

EVANS: Bergen Evans and Cornelia Evans. *A Dictionary of Contemporary American Usage*, New York, Random House, 1957.

Ferry, Ian Fletcher & Jeff (September 12, 2010). "America Was Founded as a Protectionist Nation". *Huff Post*. Retrieved February 21, 2019.

Festus P. Summers. *William L. Wilson and Tariff Reform, a Biography* (1953).

Filibuster and Cloture Retrieved from http://www.senate.gov/artandhistory/history/common/briefing/Filibuster_Cloture.htm

"Filibuster and Cloture". United States Senate. Retrieved March 5, 2010.

"Founders Online: Thomas Jefferson to Benjamin Austin, 9 January 1816". Founders.archives.gov. Retrieved February 21, 2019.

Frank William Taussig (1931). *The Tariff History of the United States*. pp. 192, 293. ISBN 9781610163309.

F. W. Taussig, "The McKinley Tariff Act." *The Economic Journal* (1891) 1#2 pp: 326–350. in JSTOR.

F. W. Taussig. *The Tariff History of The United States, 1909 edition*, p. 259.

Gary Chaison (2005). *Unions in America*. SAGE. p. 151. ISBN 9781452239477.

"George Washington: First Annual Message to Congress on the State of the Union". Presidency.ucsb.edu. Retrieved January 4, 2017.

Gold, Martin B. and Gupta, Dimple (Winter 2005). "The Constitutional Option to Change the Senate Rules and Procedures: A Majoritarian Means to Overcome the Filibuster" (PDF). *Harvard Journal of Law & Public Policy*. 28 (1): 262–64. Retrieved July 1, 2010.

Gold, Martin (2008). *Senate Procedure and Practice* (2nd ed.). Rowman & Littlefield. p. 49. ISBN 978-0-7425-6305-6. OCLC 220859622. Retrieved March 3, 2009.

"Government Tax and Revenue Chart: United States 1840-1861 - Federal State Local Data". Usgovernmentrevenue.com. Retrieved February 21, 2019.

Gregory Wallace. "Voter turnout at 20-year low in 2016," *CNN*, November 30, 2016, available at http://www.cnn.com/2016/11/11/politics/popular-vote-turnout-2016/index.html.

H. Wayne Morgan. *From Hayes to McKinley: National Party Politics, 1877–1896* (1969).

H. Wayne Morgan. *William McKinley and His America* (1965).

Hall, Peter A., and David Soskice, eds., 2001, *Varieties of Capitalism: The Institutional Foundations of Comparative Advantage* (New York: Oxford University Press).

Halstead, Murat; Munson, Augustus J. (February 21, 2019). "Life and distinguished services of William McKinley: our martyr President". Memorial Association. Retrieved February 21, 2019 – via Google Books.

Halstead, Murat; Munson, Augustus J. (January 1, 1901). *Life and distinguished services of William McKinley: Our Martyr President.* Memorial Association.

Harmonized Tariff Schedule [1] Accessed 12 Jul 2011.

Harold U. Faulkner. *Politics, Reform, and Expansion, 1890–1900* (1959).

Hill, William (1892). "Colonial Tariffs". *Quarterly Journal of Economics*. 7 (1): 78–100. JSTOR 1883762.

Hiscox, Michael (2006). "Through a Glass and Darkly: Attitudes Toward International Trade and the Curious Effects of Issue Framing". International Organization.

Hugh Tulloch (1999). *The Debate On the American Civil War Era*. Manchester UP. p. 226. ISBN 9780719049385.

"In US, Record-High 72% See Foreign Trade as Opportunity". Gallup.com. Retrieved April 22, 2018.

Irwin, Douglas A. (October 24, 2017). *Peddling Protectionism: Smoot-Hawley and the Great Depression*. Princeton University Press. ISBN 9781400888429. Retrieved February 21, 2019 – via Google Books.

Jackie Zubrzycki, "Thirteen States Now Require Grads to Pass Citizenship Test," *Education Week*, June 7, 2016, available at http://blogs.edweek.org/edweek/curriculum/2016/06/ fourteen_states_now_require_gr.html.

Jefferson, Thomas (January 9, 1816). "Letter to Benjamin Austin, Jan 9, 1816". *Boston Independent Chronicle*.

Joanne R. Reitano, *The Tariff Question in the Gilded Age: The Great Debate of 1888* (Penn State Press, 1994).

John Ashworth (1987). *'Agrarians' and 'Aristocrats': Party Political Ideology in the United States, 1837–1846*. Cambridge University Press. p. 252. ISBN 9780521335676.

John H. Barton, Judith L. Goldstein, Timothy E. Josling, and Richard H. Steinberg. *The Evolution of the Trade Regime: Politics, Law, and Economics of the GATT and the WTO* (2008).

John W. Tyler, *Smugglers and Patriots: Boston Merchants and the Advent of the American Revolution* (1986) online review.

Joseph Kahne, "Why Are We Teaching Democracy Like a Game Show?" *Education Week*, April 21, 2015, available at https://www.edweek.org/ew/articles/2015/04/22/why-arewe-teaching-democracy-like-a.html.

Karoun Demirjian (January 24, 2013). "Senate approves modest, not sweeping, changes to the filibuster". *Las Vegas Sun*. Retrieved January 31, 2013.

Kemp, Jack (November 15, 2004). "Force a real filibuster, if necessary". Townhall. Retrieved March 1, 2010.

Keith Bradsher (November 30, 1997). "Light Trucks Increase Profits But Foul Air More than Cars". *The New York Times*.

Kenneth F. Warren (2008). Encyclopedia of U.S. Campaigns, Elections, and Electoral Behavior. Sage Publications. p. 358. ISBN 9781412954891.

"Kicking Away the Ladder: The "Real" History of Free Trade - FPIF". Fpif.org. December 30, 2003. Retrieved March 3, 2018.

Kirkpatrick, David D. (April 23, 2005). "Cheney Backs End of Filibustering". *The New York Times*. ISSN 0362-4331. Retrieved January 23, 2017.

Klein, E. (2012, May 15)."Is the filibuster unconstitutional?". *The Washington Post*. Retrieved from http://www.washingtonpost.com/blogs/ezra-klein/post/is-the-filibusterunconstitutional/ 2012/05/15/gIQ-AYLp7QU_blog.html

Krugman, Paul and, Wells, Robin (2005). *Microeconomics*. Worth. ISBN 0-7167-5229-8.

Lincoln, Abraham (February 21, 2019). "Collected Works of Abraham Lincoln. Volume 1". Retrieved February 21, 2019.

Lind, Matthew. "Free Trade Fallacy". Prospect. Archived from the original on January 6, 2006. Retrieved January 3, 2011.

Lochhead, Carolyn (May 24, 2005). "Senate filibuster showdown averted". *San Francisco Chronicle*. Retrieved January 23, 2017.

Margot Sanger-Katz. *The New York Times*, The Upshot, Feb. 19, 2019, on Twitter at @sangerkatz.

Mariziani, Mimi and Lee, Diana (April 22, 2010). "Testimony of Mimi Marizani & Diana Lee, Brennan Center for Justice at NYU School of Law, submitted to the U.S. Senate Committee on Rules & Administration for the hearing entitled "Examining the Filibuster: History of the Filibuster 1789–2008". Examining the Filibuster: History of the Filibuster 1789–2008. United States Senate Committee on Rules & Administration. p. 5. Retrieved June 30, 2010.

Mark Thornton and Robert B. Ekelund, Jr. *Tariffs, Blockades, and Inflation: The Economics of the Civil War* (2004).

Maurice Allais (December 5–11, 2009). "Lettre aux français : contre les tabous indiscutés" (PDF) (in French). Marianne. p. 38.

McKinley, William (January 1, 1893). Speeches and Addresses of William McKinley: From His Election to Congress to the Present Time. D. Appleton.

McKinley, William (March 3, 1893). Speeches and Addresses of William McKinley: From His Election to Congress to the Present Time. D. Appleton. Retrieved March 3, 2018 – via Internet Archive.

Michael Lind, "Free Trade Fallacy", New America Foundation, January 1, 2003.

Moore, John A. (2011). "The Grossest and Most Unjust Species of Favoritism: Competing Views of Republican Political Economy: The

Tariff Debates of 1841 and 1842". Essays in Economic & Business History. 29: 59–73.

National Center for State Courts, "Colorado civics education program named recipient of Sandra Day O'Connor Award for Advancement of Civics Education," Press release, January 12, 2015, available at http://www.ncsc.org/Newsroom/News-Releases/2015/Colorado-civics-program-Sandra-Day-OConnor.aspx.

"New America Foundation: article -1080- "Free Trade Fallacy" "Free Trade Fallacy" -1080-". January 6, 2006. Archived from the original on January 6, 2006. Retrieved February 21, 2019.

Note: Senator Robert C. Byrd wrote in 1980 that he and Senator Mike Mansfield instituted the "two-track system" in the early 1970s with the approval and cooperation of Senate Republican leaders while he was serving as Senate Majority Whip. (Byrd, Robert C. (1991). "Party Whips, May 9, 1980". In Wendy Wolff (ed.). The Senate 1789–1989. 2. Washington, D.C.: 100th Congress, 1st Session, S. Con. Res. 18; U.S. Senate Bicentennial Publication; Senate Document 100-20; U.S. Government Printing Office. p. 203. ISBN 9780160063916. Retrieved June 30, 2010.).

Paul H. Tedesco, Patriotism, Protection, and Prosperity: James Moore Swank, the American Iron and Steel Association, and the Tariff, 1873–1913 (Garland, 1985.)

Paul Studenski; Herman Edward Krooss (2003). Financial History of the United States. Beard Books. p. 157. ISBN 9781587981753.

Piketty, Thomas, 2014, Capital in the Twenty-First Century (Cambridge, Massachusetts: Belknap Press).

Poll: Narrow majority favors 'Medicare for All' BY NATHANIEL WEIXEL - 01/30/20 01:45 PM EST. Senate Historical Office.

"Precedence of motions (Rule XXII)". Rules of the Senate. United States Senate. Archived from the original on January 31, 2010. Retrieved January 21, 2010.

"Public Trust in Government: 1958–2017," May 3, 2017, available at http://www.peoplepress. org/2017/05/03/public-trust-in-government-1958-2017/.

Rajan, Raghuram, and Luigi Zingales, 2003, Saving Capitalism from the Capitalists: Unleashing the Power of Financial Markets to Create

Wealth and Spread Opportunity (New York: Crown Publishing Group).

"Remarks by President Trump in Joint Address to Congress". white-house.gov. February 28, 2017. Retrieved March 24, 2017.

"Resolution to amend Rule XXII of the Standing Rules of the Senate". The Library of Congress. January 14, 1975. Retrieved February 18, 2010.

Retrieved March 1, 2010. Discussing Wawro, Gregory John; Schickler, Eric (2006). filibuster: obstruction and lawmaking in the U.S. Senate. Princeton, N.J.: Princeton University Press. p. 19. ISBN 978-0-691-12509-1.

Richard Hofstadter, "The Tariff Issue on the Eve of the Civil War", The American Historical Review (1938) 44#1 pp. 50–55 full text in JSTOR.

Richard Lee Colvin, "Creating capital citizens: César Chávez Public Charter Schools for Public Policy and civic education" (Washington: American Enterprise Institute, 2013), available at http://www.aei.org/publication/creating-capital-citizens-cesar-chavezpublic-charter-schools-for-public-policy-and-civic-education/.

Robert Maranto. "In Service of Citizenship: Yes Prep Public Schools and Civic Education" (Washington: American Enterprise Institute, 2017), available at http://www.aei.org/wp-content/uploads/2013/04/-in-ser-vice-of-citizenship-civic-educationand-yes-prep-public-schools_092443220200.pdf.

Roth, M. (2012, April 8). "Senate filibuster no longer requires long floor speech." Pittsburgh Post-Gazette. Retrieved from http://www.post-ga-zette.com/stories/news/us/senatefilibuster-no-longer-requires-long-floor-speech-630507/

Rybicki E. (2013). Changes to Senate Procedures in the 113th Congress Affecting the Operation of Cloture (S.Res. 15 and S.Res. 16). Congressional Research Service.

Safire, William (March 20, 2005). "Nuclear Options". The New York Times. ISSN 0362-4331. Retrieved January 23, 2017.

Sarah D. Sparks, "Community Service Requirements Seen to Reduce Volunteering," Education Week, August 20, 2013, available at https://www.edweek.org/ew/articles/2013/08/21/01volunteer_ep.h33.html.

Schlesinger, Robert (January 25, 2010). "How the Filibuster Changed and Brought Tyranny of the Minority". Politics & Policy. *U.S. News & World Report*. Retrieved June 24, 2010.

Scott C. James and David E. Lake, "The second face of hegemony: Britain's repeal of the Corn Laws and the American Walker Tariff of 1846", International Organization, Winter 1989, Vol. 43, Issue 1, pp. 1–28.

"Senate Action on Cloture Motions". United States Senate. Retrieved March 23, 2019. Erlich, Aaron (November 18, 2003). "Whatever Happened to the Old-Fashioned Jimmy Stewart-Style Filibuster?". HNN: George Mason University's History News Network. Retrieved June 30, 2010.

"Senate Rules Committee Holds Series of Hearings on the Filibuster". In The News. United States Senate Committee on Rules & Administration. June 9, 2010. Retrieved July 2, 2010.

Slade, Rachel. "The Most Powerful New Voting Bloc in America Doesn't Vote." Medium. GEN, September 13, 2018. https://gen.medium.com/ruined-entire-generation-of-young-voters-gen-z-politics-democracy-140d9ead1fa2.

Solvick, Stanley D. (1963). "William Howard Taft and the Payne-Aldrich Tariff". Mississippi Valley Historical Review. 50 (3): 424–42. JSTOR 1902605.

Springer, ed., William M. (1892). "Tariff reform, the paramount issue: Speeches and writings on the questions involved in the presidential contest of 1892." p. 391.

Srivastava, Spriha (January 24, 2017). "Trump's protectionism may hit emerging markets but not China". Cnbc.com. Retrieved March 24, 2017.

Stanley Coben, "Northeastern Business and Radical Reconstruction: A Re-Examination." Mississippi Valley Historical Review (1959): 67–90. in JSTOR.

"Support for free trade agreements rebounds modestly, but wide partisan differences remain". Pew Research.

Swedberg1, Richard (2018). "Folk economics and its role in Trump's presidential campaign: an exploratory study". Theory and Society.

Temin, Peter (October 8, 1991). "Lessons from the Great Depression". MIT Press. ISBN 9780262261197. Retrieved February 21, 2019 – via Google Books.

"The Battle for the Constitution," in partnership with the National Constitution Center. Dr. Benishek: Filibuster reform key to end gridlock in Congress. [Press release] Retrieved from http://benishek. house.gov/press-release/dr-benishek-%E2%80%9Cfilibuster-reform-keyending- gridlock-congress%E2%80%9D

"The GOP's Foolish Accommodation of Trump on Trade". *National Review*. Retrieved March 24, 2017.

The Nation's Report Card, "2014 Civics Assessment," available at https://www. nationsreportcard.gov/hgc_2014/#civics (last accessed February 2018).

The treachery of the lites Elite sense of irresponsibility. Independent. co.uk. March 10, 1995. Retrieved March 3, 2018.

Thomas J. Pressly. "Andrew Johnson and Reconstruction (review)" Civil War History (1961) 7#1 pp. 91–92 online.

Tom E. Terrill, The Tariff, Politics, and American Foreign Policy 1874– 1901 (1973)

Understanding the Filibuster: Purpose and History of the Filibuster. No Labels. Byrd, Robert C. (April 22, 2010). "Statement of U.S. Senator Robert C. Byrd, Senate Committee on Rules and Administration, "Examining the Filibuster: History of the Filibuster 1789–2008."

U.S. Census Bureau, "Voting and Registration in the Election of November 2016," Table 4c, May 2017, available at https://census.gov/ data/tables/time-series/demo/voting-andregistration/p20-580.html.

"U.S. Senate: Filibuster and Cloture". www.senate.gov. Retrieved December 13, 2016. Pildes, Rick (December 24, 2009). "The History of the Senate Filibuster". Balkinization.

Wawro, Gregory J. (April 22, 2010). "The Filibuster and Filibuster Reform in the U.S. Senate, 1917–1975; Testimony Prepared for the Senate Committee on Rules and Administration". Examining the Filibuster: History of the Filibuster 1789–2008. United States Senate Committee on Rules & Administration. Retrieved July 1, 2010.

William McKinley speech, Oct. 4, 1892 in Boston, MA William McKinley Papers (Library of Congress)

William Smith McClellan (1912)." Smuggling in the American colonies at the outbreak of the Revolution: with special reference to the West Indies trade". pp. full text online.

Woodrow Wilson: "Address to a Joint Session of Congress on the Banking System," June 23, 1913. Online by Gerhard Peters and John T. Woolley, The American Presidency Project. http://www.presidency.ucsb.edu/ws/index.php?pid=65369.

(2012, January 28). "Filibustering nominees must end." *The New York Times*. Retrieved from http://www.nytimes.com/2012/01/29/opinion/sunday/filibustering-nominees-must-end.html Smith, J. (2010, December 17). Majority does not rule in filibuster-filled 111th Congress. National Journal. Retrieved from http://www.nationaljournal.com/daily/majoritydoes-not-rule-in-filibuster-filled-111th-congress-20101216

www.ingramcontent.com/pod-product-compliance
Lightning Source LLC
Chambersburg PA
CBHW070948200526
45161CB00001BA/38